What Is the State of Human Rights?

What Is the State of Human Rights?

Other books in the At Issue series:

At ✳ Issue

What Is the State of Human Rights?

Tom Head, *Book Editor*

Bruce Glassman, *Vice President*
Bonnie Szumski, *Publisher*
Helen Cothran, *Managing Editor*

GREENHAVEN PRESS
An imprint of Thomson Gale, a part of The Thomson Corporation

THOMSON
™
GALE

Detroit • New York • San Francisco • San Diego • New Haven, Conn.
Waterville, Maine • London • Munich

THOMSON
™
GALE

323.097 HEA 2006

What is the state of human rights?

For more information, contact
Greenhaven Press
27500 Drake Rd.
Farmington Hills, MI 48331-3535
Or you can visit our Internet site at http://www.gale.com

LIBRARY OF CONGRESS CATALOGING-IN-PUBLICATION DATA
What is the state of human rights? / Tom Head, book editor.
p. cm. — (At issue)
Includes bibliographical references and index.
ISBN 0-7377-2438-2 (lib. : alk. paper) — ISBN 0-7377-2439-0 (pbk. : alk. paper)
1. Human rights—United States. 2. Human rights. I. Head, Tom. II. At issue
(San Diego, Calif.)
JC599.U5W43 2006
323'.0973—dc22   2005046104

Printed in the United States of America

Contents

Introduction

Human rights are difficult to define. For most of human history, no formal concept of human rights as such existed. Rulers could be just or unjust, and would be remembered as such, but the idea of natural rights—rights that individual human beings have whether rulers say that they have them or not—is a relatively recent idea. It was formulated primarily in the Enlightenment, a philosophical movement in eighteenth-century Europe that called greater attention to natural rights, free thought, and the value of individuals. Among the earliest and most influential of the Enlightenment thinkers was the British political philosopher John Locke, whose idea of natural rights would determine that of the U.S. government:

> Reason . . . teaches all mankind, who will but consult it, that being all and independent, no one ought to harm another in his life, health, liberty or possessions. For men being all the workmanship of one omnipotent and infinitely wise Maker . . . they are his property whose workmanship they are . . . [and] there cannot be supposed any such subordination among us that may authorize us to destroy one another, as if we were made for one another's uses.

Founding father Thomas Jefferson used this precise argument in the U.S. Declaration of Independence when he stated that "human beings are endowed by their Creator with certain unalienable rights, that among these are life, liberty, and the pursuit of happiness." (Most other documents of the time refer to "life, liberty, and property.") This idea of natural rights—that human beings have rights at birth and are not merely granted rights by the government—is responsible for the definition of human rights as it is known today.

The right to liberty has been defended in every major United Nations human rights resolution since the UN's inception, but there is and has always been a great deal of disagreement over what constitutes liberty. During the Cold War, Communist governments did not generally allow free expression or religious liberty, under the principle that such expressions have a destabilizing effect on the government and society. North Korea still practices this principle. Meanwhile, theocracies—overtly religious governments—have always tended to dismiss liberty and emphasize purity in devotion to their faiths. Saudi Arabia, for example, is by no means a liberated country—converting from Islam to another faith is punishable by death, and the government actively censors material that its administrators find objectionable. A special agency, the Commission for the Protection of Virtue and the Prevention of Vice, is given a broad mandate to enforce religious tenets on a sometimes unwilling population.

Most people in the United States who talk about human rights refer to civil liberties, such as free speech and religious freedom. Yet there is no comprehensive list of civil liberties; Even the Bill of Rights, which explicitly protects many liberties, specifies in the Ninth Amendment that the list of rights specifically granted "shall not be construed to deny or disparage others retained by the people." The right to privacy, for example, is not specified in the Bill of Rights, but in response to privacy violations, the Supreme Court has ruled that it is implicit in other amendments. The right to move across national borders is not generally regarded as a basic civil liberty, but to deny individuals the freedom to escape across a border as refugees in cases of genocide is a clear violation of their human rights. Because liberty is the absence of oppression, a civil liberty is most clearly defined when it is violated.

Secular democracies such as the United States tend to emphasize liberty as the most important human right, and perhaps the only human right worth discussing. The U.S. victory during the Cold War essentially destroyed communism, since most formerly Communist countries abandoned their earlier tenets in favor of representative governments. Liberty has unquestionably spread—and while statistics on "free" versus "nonfree" countries are always subject to the speaker's definition, it is clear that over the past twenty-five years the number of countries whose governments at least make a sincere effort to protect basic liberties has increased by a substantial number. Those remaining countries that do not respect human liberties tend to be theocracies, and many political thinkers in the United States frame the current world debate over human rights as a debate between secular democracy and theocracy, just as the Cold War represented a debate between secular democracy and communism.

Liberty is what most people mean when they refer to human rights, but the concept of property (or of the pursuit of happiness, as Jefferson stated it) has traditionally been part of the idea of human rights. The Magna Carta of 1215, the British document granting rights to landowners, focused on property issues. There are two basic interpretations of the right to property, and in some ways they are mutually contradictory.

One interpretation states that the right to property refers to a policy of government noninterference. Conservatives in the United States tend to favor this interpretation. Someone who thinks of this right as a moral imperative to be protected from government commonly favors lower taxes, less corporate regulation, and more free trade. This interpretation states that the right to property is part of the right to liberty—it is, in effect, the right to earn money without having to worry about the government coming in and taking it away. In his first inaugural address, Jefferson seemed to speak to this interpretation: "What more is necessary to make us a happy and prosperous people? Still one thing more, fellow citizens—a wise and frugal government, which shall restrain men from injuring one another, which shall leave them otherwise free to regulate their own pursuits of industry and improvement, and shall not take from the mouth of labor the bread it has earned."

Another interpretation, affirmed by recent United Nations resolutions, sees the right to property and the pursuit of happiness as a literal right to material goods such as food, water, clothing, shelter, and medicine, and to basic services such as health care, running water, electricity—and even, arguably, Internet access. The first such resolution to clearly affirm this interpretation was the UN International Covenant on Economic, Social, and Cultural Rights of 1966: "The States Parties to the present Covenant recognize the right of everyone to an adequate standard of living for himself and his family, including adequate food, clothing and housing, and to the continuous improvement of living conditions." This interpretation of the right to property reflects a policy of government intervention. According to this interpretation of human rights, governments have a moral responsibility to feed, clothe, shelter, and otherwise take care of their suffering and economically disadvantaged citizens.

These two interpretations clash in a fairly natural way: In order to take care of its citizens, a government must collect more revenue through taxes. In order to fulfill one interpretation of human rights, the government must fail according to another. Most human rights controversies can essentially be reduced to a conflict of this nature. Even theocratic governments accept some version of human rights—suppressing liberty, for example, in favor of sparing citizens eternal punishment in the afterlife. Communist governments sacrifice liberty in exchange for stability and the goal of equitable property distribution. In most cases, the conflict over human rights is not really about whether people have rights. It is, instead, a debate about what human rights are.

1

Sweatshops Violate Human Rights

Anna Yesilevsky

Anna Yesilevsky is a student at Harvard University. Her essay, excerpted below, placed in the American Humanist Association's 2004 Humanist Essay Contest for Young Women and Men of North America.

Sweatshops are a serious global human rights issue and must be dealt with by government authorities. Organized boycotts are ineffective in confronting the problem of sweatshops because they cannot be effectively used to punish any single manufacturer for rights violations. Those who support sweatshops are wrongheaded as well. Although sweatshop income may indeed be necessary for workers to support their families, this creates an exploitative and completely unacceptable "work-or-die" labor model under which manufacturers may in effect hold their workers' lives hostage. The U.S. government should deal with manufacturers that abuse labor standards by preventing the importation of their goods into the United States, thus forcing manufacturers to improve labor standards in order to remain competitive in the global market.

Oscar Wilde, in his fairy tale, "The Young King," tells the story of the main character who, on the eve of his coronation, has three terrible dreams. He sees gaunt and sickly children crowded together in a large room weaving his robe, their hands red with blood. He sees slaves thrown overboard to hunt for pearls to decorate his scepter and men dying of plague in the wilderness while seeking rubies fit for his crown. Upon awakening, he refuses to put on the costly garments that have been fashioned for him:

> Take these things away, and hide them from me.
> Though it be the day of my coronation, I will not
> wear them. For on the loom of Sorrow, and by the
> white hands of Pain, has this my robe been woven.
> There is Blood in the heart of the ruby, and Death
> in the heart of the pearl.

In discovering the cruel practices that are involved in the production of his costly raiment, the young king engages in a relatively common practice: he boycotts. Like the young king, many Americans also adopt this practice when they realize that real-life sweatshops have practices horrible enough to be relegated to the realm of nightmares.

Indeed, boycotting may seem like the correct and moral solution.

Some however consider such agitation to be ill thought out and ultimately a hindrance to the very people it tries to help. Nicholas Kristoff and Sheryl Wudunn in their *New York Times* article "Two Cheers for Sweatshops" (September 24, 2000) assert that boycotting fails to improve working conditions and instead causes sweatshops to close and workers to be fired altogether.

These are powerful contentions. However, neither viewpoint fully addresses all of the moral, ethical, and economic dilemmas that sweatshops present. Neither position goes far enough to redeem the dignity of the people harmed by sweatshops nor do they offer a solution substantially extensive and lasting. The number of flaws present in both the pro- and the anti-boycotting viewpoints presents the need for an alternative solution that goes further in agitating for positive, lasting change in the condition of the sweatshop workers.

The Trouble with Boycotts

Those who assert that boycotting is the correct answer certainly make a strong emotional appeal. After all, the status of some sweatshops is so dubious as to be called modern slavery by the American Anti Slavery Organization. Sweatshops sometimes operate using force and have conditions so dire as to be capable of causing lasting physical and emotional harm. In "Slavery: Worldwide Evil," posted on *iAbolish.com*, Charles Jacobs writes:

Locked in a room and given no food until he agreed to weave on the looms, Santosh made Oriental carpets for nine years, working from 4:00 in the morning to 11:00 at night, every day, without breaks. He was never given a single rupee for his labor. When he cut his finger with a sharp tool, the loom master shaved match heads into the cut and set the sulfur on fire. He didn't want the child's blood staining the carpet.

Though most sweatshops stop short of such wholesale abuse, work conditions are undeniably poor and human rights violations are rampant. Workers suffer from dangerous equipment and safety procedures are few or nonexistent. Hours are long and the work week is a full six or seven days. But agitating for better conditions results in termination of employment. Thus, given no leverage for negotiations and few economic alternatives, workers are forced to accept the sweatshop lifestyle or suffer even more abject poverty.

> *The status of some sweatshops is so dubious as to be called modern slavery by the American Anti Slavery Organization.*

Such conditions are not only tragic, they are an affront to human dignity and an extensive violation of human rights. There are no words strong enough to condemn practices which exploit human beings to the point of depriving them of their humanity. Seeing these things or even merely reading about them can cause a strong emotional reaction. It is very easy to react as the young king does, by refusing to use any objects created by so much suffering. However, this gut response only serves to placate the conscience without necessarily alleviating the problem.

The results of boycotting are dubious at best. Boycotters insist that the ills of sweatshops can be fixed by refusing to purchase products made in them. The owners of the sweatshops, they reason, will see that their products aren't being purchased and, succumbing to this economic coercion, will make the necessary changes to render their factories more safe, friendly, and considerate work environments. Kristoff and Wudunn explain, however, that when boycotts occur, rather than fixing conditions in sweatshops, large corporations will often shift production away entirely from countries with sweatshops, resulting in a loss of jobs for workers.

Furthermore, even if a boycott is capable of being effective, boycotters often have limited organization. This creates problems in determining a clear idea of what would constitute success. For instance, how is a sweatshop defined? Which practices are classified as being absolutely intolerable? What are the boycotters' explicit aims? Because a boycott is, in its very nature, a grassroots movement, it is often a more successful tool when a clear-cut target is easily defined.

> *There are no words strong enough to condemn practices which exploit human beings to the point of depriving them of their humanity.*

For example, there was recently a mass boycott of Abercrombie & Fitch because that company had been selling T-shirts depicting Asian-Americans in what was recognized as a very racist manner. Shortly after the boycott started, Abercrombie issued a statement apologizing for the shirts and ceased their sales. In this case the boycott was an effective tool because there was a clear target goal upon which it was easy for the boycotters to agree. The boycotters were all aware when the goal was reached because the issue of the boycott directly affected their lives.

However, in order to alter the situation of workers in sweatshops, those engaged in the boycott would first have to agree on what specific measure of standards would guarantee success and then find some mechanism for oversight that would allow them to ascertain when that level of success had been reached. Participation in boycotts is spontaneous and voluntary, two factors which allow corporations to take advantage of boycotters. And because sweatshops are located far from the country in which the goods are actually sold, multinational corporations are enabled to escape oversight. They may, in fact, claim that they have made the required changes when in actuality they haven't. Getting proof is difficult and, by the time it is available, the boycott has often run out of steam.

No Easy Solution

Thus more organization is needed to effect change than a simple boycott. Though there is contradictory evidence that boycotts do sometimes produce positive results . . . boycotting alone isn't the right answer. Results for the workers are mixed at best and, for each sweatshop victory, Kristoff and Wudunn point out that there are people whose lives are worsened when the sole effect is simply to cause a shift in production. Some corporations have been known to respond to allegations of using sweatshops by simply becoming more secretive and covert but refusing to change their methods.

Yet the laissez-faire answer that Kristoff and Wudunn provide isn't any more satisfactory. Sweatshops, they explain, actually offer workers in poor countries a path to prosperity. Workers like the opportunities that sweatshops provide: pay is higher than at any alternative job and the money earned allows them to purchase medicines, send children to school, and engage in spending which will rejuvenate their country's economy. Hence, the best way to improve the conditions found in sweatshops is simply to purchase more products made in them, not less.

> *More organization is needed to effect change than a simple boycott.*

This justification, however, lacks empirical support. After all, what incentive would companies have to change their practices if the path to profit maximization lay in minimizing labor costs? A strong force would be required to keep these capitalistic impulses in check. Furthermore, sweatshops will often engage in deceptive practices, such as lending on credit, which results in virtual entrapment for the workers who can never make enough money to pay off their debts. . . .

It isn't clear whether third world economies would be better off without sweatshops entirely. But the lesser-of-two-evils argument being used here to encourage people to consume more sweatshop-produced goods is inherently flawed. It is interesting that both of the options for dealing with sweatshops are relatively easy fixes from the standpoint of the typical concerned American: they require nothing more than a slight alteration of one's spending habits. What one gets in return seems to be an easy conscience—the belief that one is doing one's part to rid the world of labor injustices.

> **❝** *Our duty to our fellow human beings is to strive for a world where everyone is guaranteed dignity.* **❞**

However, in placating oneself by saying that either boycotting or purchasing sweatshop-made goods ultimately somehow improves the condition of sweatshop laborers, one is essentially allowing a condition of slavery to exist because it seems that the alternative is death. Our duty to our fellow human beings is to strive for a world where everyone is guaranteed dignity. This is the key value that we should strive to uphold in selecting our response to the problem of sweatshops. It may seem as though we are being forced to pick between two ills. Using empirical arguments, one may even be convinced into believing that taking one route over another will eventually lead to an improvement in the condition of the workers. But we have a duty to our fellow human beings to seek to establish a global society where things like economic servitude and human rights violations don't exist, and where each person is free to live out the course of his or her life without these limitations. As such, we can't be content with employing only economic means.

Government Intervention

Hence, the alternative I propose is to concentrate on neither boycotting goods nor purchasing them but rather in appealing to the U.S. government to pass laws prohibiting companies which sell products in American markets from violating human rights in the production of their goods. The best way to bring about lasting change is legally. Americans abroad are prohibited from committing certain acts that, while legal abroad are illegal at home. This prohibition stems from moral scruples. For instance, an American in a Middle Eastern brothel is prohibited from purchasing a child prostitute. Why can't we use the same reasoning and logic to prohibit corporations from employing labor practices abroad which don't conform to American standards of workplace safety and human rights? After all, one of the key goals of American foreign policy is the protection of human rights. Thus we should prevent corporations which violate such rights from doing business in the United States.

As our world becomes increasingly interconnected, it is necessary to maintain our principles. We can't allow ourselves to be satisfied with empty gestures that make us feel better about ourselves without eliciting any actual change. Empathy is an important part of the process, but empathy is useless without action. To say that helping workers abroad is done by taking small steps at home is a wonderful way to garner publicity, but without a coherent, organized movement that ultimately culminates in legal change, it is impossible to guarantee all people the human dignity to which they ultimately have a birthright.

2

Sweatshops Improve the Lives of Workers in Developing Nations

Jonah Goldberg

Jonah Goldberg is a nationally syndicated columnist and editor of the National Review Online.

Americans rely on low-cost goods imported from other countries. The low price of these goods is due, in part, to the extremely low wages that many overseas companies pay their employees. Factories that pay employees poorly, and often treat them poorly in other respects, are called sweatshops. Many Americans have advocated boycotting goods made in sweatshops, but the truth is that those working in sweatshops would not do so if better jobs were available to them. Sweatshops provide an income to the employees, and depriving sweatshop laborers of their jobs through boycotts forces them even further into grinding poverty. While dangerous or especially oppressive sweatshops should be shut down, most sweatshops actually improve the lives of those living in their communities and are necessary to the process of industrializing the developing world.

The lefty [liberal] ideal used to be "from each according to his ability, to each according to his need." But with the end of the Cold War, pragmatism has conquered, and the goal is now slightly less ambitious: to make labor "sweat-free." Work's okay, but sweaty work—forget it.

The anti-sweatshop movement has a lot riding on it. Everyone from [political philosopher and linguist] Noam Chomsky to [union leader] John Sweeney thinks it could form the basis for a new Left-progressive united front. Currently the coalition is driven by students, funded by unions, and cheered on by a very broad assortment of liberals.

And once you start reading the anti-sweatshop "literature," it's easy to see why the cause is so fashionable. Sweatshops are seen as spores of capitalism and Western imperialism, floating on the international trade winds, setting roots in virgin territories, and mushrooming into everything [liberal magazine] *Mother Jones* readers deplore: the oppression of women and minorities, exploitation of the poor, and destruction of the environment. What could be more useful for recharging the batteries of dour feminists and moth-balled Marxists?

The Development of the Anti-Sweatshop Movement

In the U.S., it all got started in earnest in 1997, when a bunch of kids at Duke University were determined to make sure that no Blue Devil [mascot] sweatshirts or beer cozies were made by poor people or the children of poor people. So they had a sit-in. The school administration (surprise!) caved, agreeing to require that school licensees sign a "code of conduct" permitting only "sweat-free" sweatshirts.

> *No one should defend the horrors . . . but the fact remains that, on the whole, what most opponents call 'sweatshops' are actually a good thing.*

Since then, the movement has grown to more than 100 campuses and is already of a scale comparable to the South African "divestiture" movement on campuses in the 1980s [protesting racial apartheid]. Indeed, "sweatshop" has replaced "children" as the new Swiss Army all-purpose word for the Left. In the past, any cause—gun control, welfare, Head Start, the designated-hitter rule—became immediately sacrosanct if you just rubbed it with a kid. Now "sweatshop" has a similar elastic utility. "Sweatshops are more than just labor abuse," explains Sweatshops.org, a web clearinghouse for the sweat-free movement. "When you find a sweatshop you'll also find social injustice, poverty, discrimination, abuse of women and environmental damage." In other words, everyone in the coalition of the oppressed can get a treat by whacking this pinata.

> **❝** *All of the Asian economic powers began with sweaty labor, which generated the resources to create a less sweaty economy.* **❞**

As Walter Olson of the Manhattan Institute has catalogued, just about anything can be called a sweatshop now. In 1999, AFL-CIO executive vice-president Linda Chavez-Thompson received raucous applause from marchers when she declared that Yale University was a "sweatshop"—because it refused to permit its "exploited" grad students to unionize. (They get paid close to $40,000 at an annualized rate, plus free tuition and health insurance.) *Time* magazine called the dot-com companies a "a piecework-industry sweatshop." Dan Stein, head of the anti-immigration group FAIR [Federation for American Immigration Reform], declared that a bill granting more U.S. visas to high-skilled computer programmers and engineers "should rightly be called the Silicon Valley Sweatshop Act." (In 1998, salaries for software engineers started at $50,000 a year; hardly something for Upton Sinclair to break his pencil about.)

The real villains, of course, are the Third World enterprises where poor people work long hours in unpleasant circumstances for less than a dollar an hour. No one should defend the horrors—factories with locked doors during fires, employers who confiscate passports and harass workers, etc.—but the fact remains that, on the whole, what most opponents call "sweatshops" are actually a good thing.

Imposing Western Values

A recent *Lingua Franca* cover story surveyed the current state of the academic debate over sweatshops, and found that even the most rabid critics are forced to concede that the evil multinationals generally pay at least the prevailing wage in the countries in which they operate, and, more often than not, more. Most of the "exploitees" are happy to get these jobs because, as Columbia University economist Jagdish Bhagwati put it, they're a "ticket to slightly less impoverishment."

Not surprisingly, this sort of pragmatism can drive a gender theorist to the point of kicking over her fern. What about the oppression? What about the racism? What about my grant to study homophobia in Indonesian sneaker factories? Indeed, most academics in the anti-sweatshop movement are cultural-studies types whose chief interest is finding new cudgels against whitey.

The broad economic consensus reaches from Bhagwati and [economist] Milton Friedman all the way over to stalwart liberals like [Harvard University president] Lawrence Summers and [journalist] Paul Krugman: Sweatshops, all in all, equal progress. Economic development makes people less poor, which means healthier, freer, and more capable of protecting the environment and workers' rights. All of the Asian economic powers began with sweaty labor, which generated the resources to create a less sweaty economy. Krugman points out, for example, that in 1975 South Korean wages equaled only 5 percent of U.S. wages; two decades later, they had risen to 43 percent.

A handful of economists dismiss this consensus, saying their colleagues aren't asking the right questions. Jeffrey Winters, a professor of political economy at Northwestern University, suggests that we should be asking, "How do wages compare with those of CEOs and celebrity endorsers?" The bottom line, Winters tells *Lingua Franca*, is that "Nike does not pay a living wage and could easily afford to."

> *What the anti-sweatshop movement amounts to is a war on development.*

The anti-imperialists are, themselves, being rather imperialistic. For someone to ask, "What would [philosopher Martin] Heidegger say about Bangladeshi piecework?" is an example of Western bias; but so is asking whether a Vietnamese worker at a Nike plant is making a large enough fraction of [basketball player and Nike spokesperson] Michael Jordan's salary. In neither case does the question represent a truly "indigenous" way

24

of looking at the issue. Income inequality is something that particularly offends Western sensibilities.

> ❝ *Sweatshops are not an end in themselves, but the first rung on the ladder of success.* ❞

Winters asks, "Should American students be any less outraged just because Nike positions itself slightly higher than some of the exceptionally bad local Indonesian or Vietnamese producers?" The answer, of course, is yes—they should be less outraged, though they can still be angry. If Nike is raising the standard of living and bringing thousands of jobs that wouldn't otherwise be available to a poor country, then maybe outrage isn't the right response. As Linda Lim, a professor at the University of Michigan and a critic of the sweat-free cause, told *Lingua Franca*, this is "patronizing white-man's-burden stuff."

The Long-Term Benefits of Sweatshops

To the anti-sweat ideologues, Western-style capitalism is an unnatural imposition of alien values on foreign cultures, but somehow the imposition of equally Western concepts of fair labor practices and just compensation are wholly consistent with these cultures. Take child labor: It may be horrifying to Americans who treat their progeny as opportunities to display conspicuous consumption, but in much of the Third World, it is natural to view your child as an economic asset. In countries where schools are not available or affordable, it would be limousine liberalism on a global scale to insist that children stay home and consume resources—which is why even the U.N. and most nongovernment organizations oppose an outright ban on child labor.

What the anti-sweatshop movement amounts to is a war on development. And while the motives of the students who form the backbone of the movement are surely decent, the intentions of their backers are less so. The United Needletrades, Industrial, and Textile Employees, a member of the AFL-CIO, has seen its membership plummet by nearly two-thirds over the last few decades largely because garment-industry jobs have gone overseas. Its effort to ban the importation of whatever it claims to be sweatshop products is directly, and often shamelessly, tied to a protectionist desire to keep out cheaper products and save union jobs.

Sweatshops are not an end in themselves, but the first rung on the ladder of success; rather than hurry nations up that ladder, radicals would keep these nations frozen in amber—living museums of poverty and ignorance. The best evidence that sweatshops are transitory in nature can be found right here at home, where the anti-sweatshop movement began with the tragic Triangle Shirtwaist fire of 1911 [in which building exits were locked and many employees perished]. Sweatshops helped move millions of unskilled immigrants out of poverty. While the fire helped galvanize reformers to curb many of the excesses of the garment industry, it was the success of the industry itself that made such efforts affordable.

Rose Freedman, the last survivor of the Triangle Shirtwaist fire, died in February at the age of 107. Mrs. Freedman, a tireless advocate for labor reforms, was a remarkable woman who saw a lot in her lifetime. But what was barely mentioned in her obituaries was that she lived to see her granddaughter become the president of 20th Century Fox Television.

If that's the kind of intractable intergenerational poverty that sweatshops propagate, then the rest of the world needs more of them.

3

The U.S. Detainment of Prisoners at Guantánamo Bay Violates Human Rights

Amnesty International

Founded in 1962, Amnesty International is a leading international human rights organization. With over 1.8 million members and chapters in 150 countries, it monitors treatment of prisoners and oppressed groups under governments around the world.

The United States has imprisoned hundreds of al Qaeda terrorists and members of Afghanistan's Taliban regime in a U.S. military prison in Guantánamo Bay, Cuba, in response to the terrorist attacks of September 11, 2001 (in which al Qaeda terrorists hijacked airplanes and crashed them into the World Trade Center and Pentagon), and the subsequent Afghanistan War. The prisoners were classified as enemy combatants and were initially denied access to lawyers. Most are charged in executive military commissions, which do not have the same standards as traditional courtroom trials. The United States has also mistreated prisoners by using interrogation techniques that may qualify as torture. The United States should not violate human rights as part of its war on terror.

[In early 2002] President George W. Bush signed a Military Order on the Detention, Treatment and Trial of Certain Non-

Citizens in the War Against Terrorism. Anyone held under the Military Order can be detained indefinitely without charge or trial. They can also be brought to trial by military commissions—executive bodies, not independent or impartial courts—whose verdicts, including death sentences, cannot be appealed in any court. Despite widespread international condemnation of these proposed trials, the US authorities have continued preparations for them . . .

Amnesty International has called for the Military Order to be rescinded ever since it was signed, on the grounds that it is fundamentally flawed and because trials under its provisions will violate international fair trial standards [because]:

• The commissions will entirely lack independence from the executive.

• The right to counsel of choice and to an effective defence is severely restricted.

• There will be no right of appeal to an independent and impartial court established by law.

• Only foreign nationals are eligible for such trials, violating the prohibition on the discriminatory application of fair trial rights. A US citizen charged with a similar crime would not face trial by military commission, and would have the right to appeal to higher courts of Law.

The Military Order can be applied to anyone suspected of being or having knowingly harboured either a member of [terrorist group] *al-Qa'ida* or someone who has "engaged in, aided or abetted, or conspired to commit, acts of international terrorism." It is broad in scope and open-ended. The Pentagon's instructions for the military commissions extend the concept of armed conflict to include single hostile acts or attempted acts, or conspiracy to carry out such acts, a definition so broad that it could encompass many acts that would normally fall under the jurisdiction of the normal criminal justice system.

A Collapsing Human Rights Record

The USA's claims to be a progressive force for human rights have rung increasingly hollow [since 2001]. The government's continuing pursuit of military commission trials against a selection of foreign nationals it . . . unilaterally labelled as "enemy combatants" and held in virtual incommunicado detention for more than two years [has fed] a growing recognition that this is an administration which refuses to place respect for human rights at the heart of its response to the atrocities of 11 September 2001.

Double standards are apparent. On the one hand, the executive plans to try a selection of foreign nationals under a military commission system designed to secure convictions on lower standards of evidence than pertain in the US courts. On the other, the very same administration has discussed how any US agents accused of torture during the "war on terror" might avoid conviction. Previously secret memoranda have suggested legal defences for accused US agents of "necessity" and "self-defence," as well as the notion that authorization under the President's Commander in Chief powers could override the prohibition on torture.

> **''** We now know that the administration has approved interrogation techniques that . . . included stress positions, sensory deprivation, hooding, stripping, the use of dogs to inspire fear, and isolation. **''**

A 26 February 2002 memorandum from the Justice Department to the Pentagon describes the military commissions as "entirely creatures of the President's authority as Commander in Chief . . . and are part and parcel of the conduct of a military campaign." A few days earlier, President Bush signed a memorandum holding that this was a campaign which "requires new thinking in the law of war." The thinking that has been done, however, has resulted in familiar abuses, including the denial of *habeas corpus*, the use of incommunicado and secret detention, a pattern of official commentary on the presumed guilt of detainees, and the sanctioning of harsh interrogation techniques which contravene international standards. This rejection of basic safeguards has made torture and ill-treatment more likely to occur.

The military commissions will be able to use the fruits of any torture or ill-treatment that may have occurred. Indeed, the procedures for the commissions provide that evidence "shall" be admitted if the presiding officer or a majority of the commission members consider that it "would have probative value to a reasonable person." In other words, if a statement made under torture or coerced by the conditions of detention at Guantánamo or elsewhere is considered to have some "probative value," it "shall" be admitted. In similar vein, the Justice Department memorandum of 26 February 2002 advised that "incriminating statements may be admitted in proceedings before military commissions even if the interrogating officers do not abide by the requirements of *Miranda* [the US Supreme Court decision controlling the rights of criminal suspects and conduct of interrogators]." We now know that the administration has approved interrogation techniques that have gone beyond normal US army doctrine. The purpose of the techniques has been to extract information. Methods approved in December 2002 by Secretary Rumsfeld for use at Guantánamo, for example, included stress positions, sensory deprivation, hooding, stripping, the use of dogs to inspire fear, and isolation.

> *The use of 'extended solitary confinement in dark' cells was one of the torture techniques . . . that the US government cited in its build up to the invasion of [Iraq].*

The use of "extended solitary confinement in dark" cells was one of the torture techniques used in Iraq that the US government cited in its build up to the invasion of that country. The USA has used the same technique in occupied Iraq, systematically according to the International Committee of the Red Cross, and in Guantánamo the first six men made eligible for trial by military commission, including the four whose preliminary hearings are imminent, have been subjected to prolonged isolation. Sometime after July 2003 when the six were deemed by President Bush to fall under the Military Order, they were removed from Camp Delta—where most of the hundreds of Guantánamo detainees are held—to the isolation cells of Camp Echo. There, each has been held for months for 23–24 hours a day in a reportedly windowless cell with no possibility of communication with other detainees. Prolonged isolation in conditions of reduced sensory stimulation can cause severe physical and psychological damage. In a declaration signed on 31 March 2004, psychiatrist Dr. Daryl Matthews, who visited Guantánamo in 2003 at the invitation of the Pentagon, stated that the solitary confinement places the detainees "at significant risk for future psychiatric deterioration, possibly including the development of irreversible psychiatric symptoms." It also increases the susceptibility of the detainees to being coerced into making confessions or statements implicating themselves or others.

Administrative Review

Salim Ahmed Hamdan, a Yemeni national who has been in US custody since November 2001, was transferred to an isolation cell in Guantánamo's Camp Echo in early December 2003. According to Dr. Matthews's declaration, Salim Ahmed Hamdan said that he had "considered confessing falsely to ameliorate his situation." Two former Guantánamo detainees from the UK wrote to a US Senate Committee in May recalling: "After three months in solitary confinement under harsh conditions and repeated interrogations, we finally agreed to confess [to being present at a meeting with Osama bin Laden]. Last September an agent from MI5 [British secret service] came to Guantánamo with documentary evidence that proved we could not have been in Afghanistan at the time . . . In the end we could prove our alibis, but we worry about people from countries where records are not as available."

Salim Ahmed Hamdan, fellow Yemeni Ali Hamza Ahmed Sulayman al Bahlul, Ibrahim Ahmed Mahmoud al Qosi, a Sudanese national, and David Matthew Hicks, an Australian, are the four men who are scheduled to face preliminary hearings prior to their trials by military commission. The charges against them include conspiracy to commit war crimes and "terrorism." The death penalty will not be sought against these four men as at their actual trials the defendants will appear before a commission of five members including the "presiding office." There will also be an alternate member. A death penalty trial must be held before seven commission members. Life imprisonment will be the maximum punishment available in these four cases. Sentencing is at the discretion of the commission members. There are no detailed guidelines. The rules simply state that all sentences "should be grounded in a recognition that military commissions are a function of the President's warfighting role as Commander-in-Chief of the Armed Forces of the United States and of the broad deterrent impact associated with a sentence's effect on adherence to the laws and customs of war in general."

The time the defendants have already spent in detention "shall not be considered to fulfill any term of imprisonment imposed by a military commission." Even if a defendant is acquitted, his release is not guaranteed. If he is considered still to be a security risk or to have intelligence value, he would return to indefinite detention unless and until a Combatant Status Review Tribunal determined that he was no longer an "enemy combatant." This administrative review process is entirely separate from the military commissions. . . .

> *[Officials] in the US administration have repeatedly made it clear what they think of the detainees, and . . . undermined the presumption of innocence included in the rules for trials by military commission.*

Article 14 of the International Covenant on Civil and Political Rights (ICCPR) guarantees that "[e]veryone convicted of a crime shall have the right to his conviction and sentence being reviewed by a higher tribunal according to law." The United Nations Human Rights Committee has stated: "The provisions of article 14 apply to all courts and tribunals" and that proceedings must "genuinely afford the full guarantees stipulated in article 14." Under Article 14, therefore, the appeal court must be a competent, independent and impartial tribunal established by law. Clearly, the review panel does not meet this standard.

Undermining the Presumption of Innocence

Under the commission rules, the review panel members are selected by the Secretary of Defense, who can also remove them for "good cause," which "includes, but is not limited to, physical disability, military exigency, or other circumstances." That it is Secretary Rumsfeld who chooses review panel members was confirmed by a senior Pentagon official at a briefing in December 2003:

> Q: Who chose the review panel members?
> A: The Secretary of Defense.

This system has been crying out for a semblance of independence. Yet Secretary Rumsfeld's choice of who will serve on the review panel has already caused concern. For example, one of his appointees, former judge, prosecutor and congressman Edward George Biester, has been described as Secretary Rumsfeld's "good friend and sometime neighbour," and as an individual who is "very friendly with Rumsfeld," according to a former judicial colleague of Edward Biester. Another report states:

"Secretary of Defense Donald Rumsfeld personally named Biester to the Military Commission Review Panel. . . . It was perhaps the culmination of a friendship that stretches back more than 35 years. Biester and Rumsfeld are old friends, who first met when they served in Congress together and have stayed close over the years."

Edward Biester, and the other appointees, will be commissioned as major generals in the army and will receive military pay.

Even if the review panel was independent, its decisions with regard to the final disposition of the case, including sentencing, will only have the power of recommendation to the Secretary of Defense. The Secretary of Defense would then review the trial record and the review body's recommendation. The final decision in any case will reside with the President, the official who named the defendant eligible for trial in the first place, or, by the Secretary of Defence, if so designated by the President.

> *The US authorities justify . . . military commissions by saying that they have historically been used. This is not the claim of a government with a progressive attitude to human rights.*

These two officials and others in the US administration have repeatedly made it clear what they think of the detainees, and in so doing have undermined the presumption of innocence included in the rules for trials by military commission and much trumpeted by the Pentagon. For example, the pattern of public commentary on the cases has included the following labels being put on the Guantánamo detainees by senior members of the administration:

These people are terrorists . . . They are terrorists. They are uniquely dangerous. Attorney General John Ashcroff, 20 January 2002.

Hard-core, well-trained terrorists. Secretary of Defense Donald Rumsfeld, 20 January 2002.

Among the most dangerous, best-trained, vicious killers on the face of the earth. Secretary of Defence Donald Rumsfeld, 27 January 2002.

These are the worst of a very bad lot. They are very dangerous. They are devoted to killing millions of Americans, innocent Americans, if they can, and they are perfectly prepared to die in the effort. Vice President Dick Cheney, 27 January 2002.

These killers—these are killers. . . . These are killers. These are terrorists. President George Bush, 28 January 2002.

Remember, these are—the ones in Guantánamo Bay are killers. They don't share the same values we share. President Bush, 20 March 2002.

So they're dangerous people, whether or not they go before a military commission . . . We're dealing with a special breed of person here . . . Deputy Secretary of Defence Paul Wolfowitz, 21 March 2002.

The only thing I know for certain is that these are bad people. President Bush, 17 July 2003.

The right to the presumption of innocence requires that judges and juries refrain from prejudging any case. It also means that public authorities, not least those who have direct influence and control over proceedings, should not make statements relating to the guilt or innocence of any individual before the outcome of a trial. The UN Human Rights Committee has stated in its authoritative interpretation of the right to the presumption of innocence guaranteed under the ICCPR [International Covenant on Civil and Political Rights]: "It is . . . a duty for all public authorities to refrain from prejudging the outcome of a trial."

An Outdated Approach

Following the naming of the first six detainees under the Military Order in July 2003, the UN Special Rapporteur on the independence of judges and lawyers stated that "in proceeding to apply these drastic measures to counter terrorism, the United States Government is seen defying United Nations resolutions, including General Assembly resolution A/RES/57/219 of 18 December 2002 and Security Council resolution S/RES/1456 of 20 January 2003." The Rapporteur pointed out that these resolutions "reiterate very clearly that counter-terrorism measures must comply with international human rights law, humanitarian law and refugee law. It was the US that went to war with Iraq for breach of a Security Council resolution, and here we find the US blatantly defying these resolutions which they were party to."

> *Executive military commissions have no place in 21st century criminal justice systems.*

The US authorities justify President Bush's decision to resort to military commissions by saying that they have historically been used. This is not the claim of a government with a progressive attitude to human rights. History is full of practices which have now been left behind. The UN Human Rights Committee has stated:

> "The provisions of article 14 (of the ICCPR) apply to all courts and tribunals within the scope of that article whether ordinary or specialized. The Committee notes the existence, in many countries, of military or special courts which try civilians. This could present serious problems as far as the equitable, impartial and independent administration of justice is concerned. Quite often the reason for the establishment of such courts is to enable exceptional procedures to be applied which do not comply with normal standards of justice. While the Covenant does not prohibit such categories of courts, nevertheless the conditions which it lays down clearly indicate that the trying of civilians by such courts should be very exceptional and take place under conditions which genuinely afford the full guarantees stipulated in article 14."

On 17 August 2004, John Altenburg, the appointing authority at the Office of Military Commissions said: "This is the first time we've done commissions in 60 years, and we'll have to wait and see what happens as to how it goes and how smoothly it goes." What he failed to point out was that the creation of a separate system of trials before executive bodies is contrary to international standards. The more than half a century in which military commissions have not been used in the USA is a period that has seen the reinforcement of a broad framework of fair trial guarantees in international human rights law and standards and in international humanitarian law. Executive military commissions have no place in 21st century criminal justice systems.

4

The U.S. Detainment of Prisoners at Guantánamo Bay Is Necessary

Mark Landsbaum

Mark Landsbaum is director of Landmark Communications, a marketing company. He also has twenty-four years of experience as a journalist and frequently writes on public policy issues.

Following the terrorist attacks of September 11, 2001 (in which al Qaeda terrorists hijacked airliners and rammed them into the World Trade Center and the Pentagon), and the subsequent war in Afghanistan, the United States imprisoned hundreds of al Qaeda terrorists and members of Afghanistan's Taliban regime in a U.S. military prison in Guantánamo Bay, Cuba. The prisoners were classified as "enemy combatants" and, despite protests from international human rights groups, were denied access to lawyers. The Supreme Court later ruled that this policy was unconstitutional. In 2004 over two hundred prisoners were released due largely to the Court's ruling and the efforts of human rights activists. At least ten of those prisoners have since resumed terrorist activities. The U.S. detainment of prisoners at Guantánamo Bay is necessary because terrorists, once released, will likely continue to target Americans for death. Taliban fighters and al Qaeda terrorists do have a right to due process, but this right should not come at the expense of American lives.

Mark Landsbaum, "Released to Kill," *FrontPage Magazine*, October 27, 2004. Copyright © 2004 by the Center for the Study of Popular Culture. Reproduced by permission.

I magine capturing enemy combatants during World War II, then returning them to their homelands while the war continued to rage, simply because they promised not to fight any more.

Unlikely? Maybe during World War II—but thanks to the modern Left [liberals], this is exactly what we're doing in the War on Terror.

> **The obvious downside to releasing prisoners during war is that they potentially replenish the enemy's forces.**

More than 200 terrorist suspects held in the U.S. Navy prison at Guantanamo Bay, Cuba, have been released from custody after signing pledges renouncing violence and promising not to bear arms against U.S. forces or its allies.

Not surprisingly, U.S. military officials now concede that at least 10 of those released are believed to have broken their promises and resumed terrorist activity.

Perhaps foremost among the released prisoners is Abdullah Mehsud, 28, who after 25 months in custody at Guantanamo has used his new freedom to mastermind the kidnapping on October 9 of two Chinese involved in the building of Pakistan's Gomal Zam Dam project. One of the Chinese hostages was killed during a Pakistani rescue attempt this week. The kidnapping was Mehsud's response to ground, helicopter and artillery offensives that failed to force the tribes to hand over al-Qaeda fugitives.

Another three prisoners released from Guantanamo Bay custody are believed to have been killed after also resuming terrorist activities. One released detainee killed a judge leaving an Afghanistan mosque.

"It's a difficult balance to achieve between not wanting to hold individuals longer than is necessary and the risk to our forces if the individual returns to the fight," explained Air Force Major Michael Shavers, quoted by the *Washington Times*.

Hunting Mehsud Again

There has been pressure on the U.S. military to prevent holding prisoners "longer than is necessary" from the so-called

Center for Constitutional Rights, whose president Michael Ratner deems U.S. military tribunals that try suspected terrorists to be "kangaroo courts," lacking credibility in the Muslim world. Other "human rights" groups also have criticized the U.S. Defense Department for holding prisoners at the naval base, some for more than two years while only a few have been charged. [2004 Democratic] presidential candidate John Kerry . . . joined in the criticism of the Bush administration's handling of prisoners, claiming, "They dismiss the Geneva Convention starting in Afghanistan and Guantanamo. . . . "

The obvious downside to releasing prisoners during war is that they potentially replenish the enemy's forces. But there are also great propaganda and morale gains for the enemy when prisoners like Mehsud are freed.

> *Not only are freed prisoners . . . able now to resume terrorist activities against U.S. forces, but they also can pose disproportionate problems for U.S. allies.*

Mehsud, who now holds the notorious distinction of being Pakistan's most wanted man, is described in a report in the *London Independent* as a "growing legend" among rebel Pakistanis. The fugitive terrorist, who is suspected to have aligned with al-Qaeda since his release, was a minor player in 1996 when he lost a leg storming Kabul [Afghanistan] with the Taliban. But now the mastermind of the Chinese kidnapping has achieved a high-profile notoriety while believed to be holed up in the South Waziristan tribal region, where tribesmen and foreign fighters ferociously oppose the Pakistani army because, some believe, [terrorist leader] Osama bin Laden may be in hiding there.

While in custody, Mehsud's only audience was other prisoners. Now his high profile results in his words being repeated in press reports worldwide, giving him a prominent platform to criticize U.S. policies and to proclaim that the American presence in Iraq and Afghanistan is a provocation that must be avenged by Muslims.

Not only are freed prisoners like Mehsud able now to resume terrorist activities against U.S. forces, but they also can pose disproportionate problems for U.S. allies. Pakistanis, for instance, are mobilized with a top priority for finding, capturing or killing Mehsud, whose new status as a rebel hero inflames conditions in the region.

The *Daily News* in Islamabad, Pakistan, described Mehsud as having become "a hero to anti-U.S. fighters active in both Afghanistan and Pakistan."

"We must hunt Mehsud down. The man has got too big for his shoes," an anomymous Pakistani security official was quoted saying. Mehsud and others like him aid a new generation of guerrillas organizing and rallying supporters in remote regions beyond the reach of Pakistani authorities.

Other Former Prisoners

About 550 terror suspects remain at the Cuban prison in U.S. custody, but further releases may occur if the detainees are no longer deemed to be a threat, or no longer have intelligence value, or are not candidates for trial by military commission, according to Major Shavers. So far, the Pentagon says more than 150 have been released outright. Another 56 were transferred to the control of other governments, including 29 to Pakistan.

The Associated Press reported that Maulvi Abdel Ghaffer, a senior Taliban commander in northern Afghanistan before his 2001 capture, was released to Afghanistan after eight months at Guantanamo. Afghan leaders believe Ghaffer was heading Taliban forces in the Uruzgan province when he was killed during a raid.

> *The fact is terrorists are running free in Afghanistan and potentially more around the world because the Legal Left placed their 'inalienable rights' above the safety of Americans.*

Other former prisoners now living in Denmark and Sweden have indicated publicly they wanted to return to fighting. Slimane Hadj Abderrahmane, who was released to return to Denmark in February, later backed off his comments about going to Chechnya to fight Russians, and promised once again to honor his original promise not to take up arms. Danish authorities reportedly are keeping tabs on him. Mehdi-Muhammed Ghezali, released in July after two years at Guantanamo, is being monitored by Swedish intelligence agents, who reportedly do not consider him a threat.

Meanwhile, a military source told *Pakistan's Daily Times*, "We are closing in on Abdullah, and his days are numbered."

Latest reports are that Pakistani security forces have surrounded a village in South Waziristan where Mehsud and his men are believed to be hiding. "We are optimistic that Abdullah Mehsud would be captured soon," a government spokesman said.

One might ask whether Mehsud's re-capture or death will occur before another prisoner is released from Guantanamo to take his place in the Pakistan mountains.

The *Washington Post* reports that a federal judge ruled last week that terror suspects held in Cuba must be allowed to meet with lawyers, and their conversations cannot be monitored by the government. U.S. District Judge Colleen Kollar-Kotelly reportedly rebuked the Bush administration for "attempts to erode this bedrock principle" of attorney-client privacy. Previously, the Supreme Court had ruled that foreign-born detainees in the Navy prison camp at Guantanamo Bay could challenge their captivity in American courts.

The Defense Department said this ruling means the chance that former Guantanamo Bay prisoners might return to terrorism is unlikely to hinder the release of more prisoners.

"I don't think it will make it more difficult to release people in the future," said Pentagon spokesman Shavers, quoted by the *Washington Post*. "We will continue to apply stringent scrutiny of the cases of these individuals."

Another Pentagon spokesman offered, "[W]e can't be 100 percent sure they will not return to the fight."

As Major Shavers noted, "What people need to understand is that a number of these detainees are highly skilled in concealing the truth."

Rights and Safety

Significantly, the Israeli daily *Haaretz* last week reported of the existence of a Jordanian "ghost jail" the CIA allegedly is using to hold at least 11 senior al-Qaeda leaders, beyond the reach of the U.S. courts—and perhaps beyond the policy of releasing terror suspects who promise not to fight again.

"Their detention outside the U.S. enables CIA interrogators

to apply interrogation methods that are banned by U.S. law, and to do so in a country where co-operation with the U.S. is particularly close, thereby reducing the danger of leaks," wrote Yossi Melman, a leading authority on intelligence. There was no immediate comment from officials in Jordan, and the U.S. embassy in Jordan denied the report.

The fact is terrorists are running free in Afghanistan and potentially more around the world because the Legal Left placed their "inalienable rights" above the safety of Americans. Institutions like the Center for Constitutional Rights, the ACLU [American Civil Liberties Union], and the National Lawyers Guild do this out of a hatred of this country and all that she stands for—and in this instance, they are literally "softening us up for the kill."

5

The Patriot Act Threatens Human Rights

Timothy Lynch

Timothy Lynch is an attorney and serves as director of the Project on Criminal Justice for the Cato Institute, a libertarian public policy think tank. He is editor of After Prohibition: An Adult Approach to Drug Policies in the 21st Century *(2000), as well as numerous editorials and scholarly papers on criminal justice issues.*

In the aftermath of the terrorist attacks of September 11, 2001, in which terrorists hijacked civilian aircraft and rammed them into the World Trade Center and the Pentagon, the U.S. Congress overwhelmingly passed the USA PATRIOT Act, which was quickly signed by President George W. Bush. The act streamlines the law enforcement process when applied to terrorists. Although many provisions of the act have been widely praised, some have raised civil liberties concerns especially since the definitions of *terrorist* and *terrorist activities* remain largely up to law enforcement. Most striking is Section 215 of the act, which allows law enforcement personnel to search and seize anything they are looking for—sometimes without judicial review. The Patriot Act threatens civil liberties and clearly violates the spirit of the Fourth Amendment, bringing the United States a step closer to becoming a police state rather than a supporter of human rights.

Now that . . . years have passed since the trauma of the Sept. 11 [2001] catastrophe, it is a good time to take a step back from the politics of the moment and take stock as to how our policymakers have responded to the threat posed by terrorism.

Sending American soldiers to Afghanistan was a decisive move by President Bush—because it was going right to the root of the problem, which is [terrorist leader] Osama bin Laden, his elite henchmen and his training camps.

The war on the home front also has been aggressive but in many ways misguided.

Liberty and Privacy

The assumption has been that there was simply too much liberty and privacy in America—and that federal law-enforcement agencies did not have enough power. To remedy that perceived problem, policymakers rushed the USA Patriot Act into law.

The Patriot Act was designed to reduce privacy and increase security. It has succeeded in at least reducing privacy.

Financial privacy is essentially gone. The feds have turned banks, brokerage houses, insurers and other financial institutions into state informers. Those firms must notify the Treasury Department about "suspicious" transactions, and the government can subpoena your checking-account records even if there is no evidence of wrongdoing.

Even though the feds were notified about several of hijacker Mohammed Atta's financial transactions before Sept. 11, no action was taken.

> **❝** The Patriot Act was designed to reduce privacy and increase security. It has succeeded in at least reducing privacy. **❞**

But in the logic of the public sector, that failure means the government was hobbled by insufficient money and insufficient power. Thus, the Treasury Department is now engaging in more surveillance.

Attorney General John Ashcroft says that all of the "safeguards of our Constitution" have been honored. But the Constitution's most vital safeguard is the principle of the separation of powers, and it has been undermined repeatedly.

One of the most odious provisions of the Patriot Act is known as Section 215.

That provision empowers FBI agents to demand things from people in terrorism-related investigations.

Ashcroft and conservative analysts claim that the Patriot Act operates in a similar fashion to ordinary search warrants so there is nothing to worry about. Heather Mac Donald of the Manhattan Institute [a moderately conservative think tank], for example, says, "The FBI can do nothing under Section 215 without the approval of a federal court."

In truth, the act creates a façade of judicial review. Here is the pertinent language: "Upon an application made pursuant to this section, the judge shall enter" the order.

> *Too many conservatives have brushed aside grievances about civil-liberties violations in the mistaken belief that President Bush's political opponents are simply trying to dress up a partisan attack.*

That was crafty. Instead of enacting a law that says whenever an FBI agent wants to demand something from someone, he can do so as long as he is following leads in a terrorism investigation, the Patriot Act accomplishes the same end indirectly. The FBI can now use boilerplate forms and submit them to federal magistrates, who "shall" approve the applications.

The judicial check is not there. The judiciary cannot scrutinize the foundation for the Justice Department applications.

The impression is, in any event, false. The FBI can use Section 215 to obtain personal belongings—anything, really—directly from a person's home.

To top it all off, Section 215 has a gag provision that criminalizes speech about 215 orders. So if the CEO of a telecommunications firm finds that his company is spending a million dollars a year to comply with Section 215 orders and wants to complain to Congress, he better not make that call or send that letter. . . .

The courts are not likely to abide by that blatant restriction of free speech, but it may take years for a definitive ruling on the subject.

In the meantime, only the FBI knows how many people will have been cowed into silence by 215.

Too many conservatives have brushed aside grievances about civil-liberties violations in the mistaken belief that President Bush's political opponents are simply trying to dress up a partisan attack in noble-sounding rhetoric about liberty, privacy and the Constitution. The opposite is true.

President Bush and Attorney General Ashcroft have given their political opponents a just cause—namely, resisting the growth of a surveillance state.

6

The Patriot Act Does Not Threaten Human Rights

Kevin V. Ryan

Kevin V. Ryan is the U.S. attorney for the Northern District of California.

Congress passed the USA PATRIOT Act in response to the terrorist attacks of September 11, 2001, in which terrorists hijacked airplanes and rammed them into the World Trade Center and Pentagon, resulting in almost three thousand deaths. Although some have criticized the legislation, most do so based on a faulty understanding of its actual content. The Patriot Act was written to serve four functions: to increase U.S. law enforcement powers so that terrorist organizations can be investigated in the same way that organized crime is investigated, to increase the availability of high-technology law enforcement tools, to connect various law enforcement and intelligence agencies so that they may more effectively coordinate counterterrorist activities, and to increase the penalties for those who commit acts of terrorism. It specifically prohibits racial and religious profiling, and it cannot be used to censor free speech.

On September 11 [2001], we all bore witness to the callous viciousness of our terrorist enemies, as well as the devastation they seek to inflict. That day, more than 3,000 Americans lost their lives, and the fight against terrorism became the Justice Department's first and highest priority.

Kevin V. Ryan, "Patriot Act Is Right and Just," *Human Events Online*, www.humanev entsonline.com, September 12, 2003. Copyright © 2003 by Human Events Inc. Reproduced by permission.

Thus, when I took office as the U.S. attorney for the Northern District of California in July 2002, I immediately mandated that the highest priority of my office would be the protection of this district from a terrorist attack. I have instructed my prosecutors to use every legal weapon at their disposal to fight the war against terrorism particularly the USA Patriot Act.

> *While the Patriot Act is a key tool in the fight against terrorism, it . . . simply took existing legal principles and retrofitted them for the challenges posed by a well-financed and highly coordinated global terrorist network.*

Unfortunately, a small but vocal group of protesters has been mounting a campaign against the Patriot Act. Swayed by these protesters, a few local city councils have passed resolutions opposing the Patriot Act, including the San Francisco Board of Supervisors, which approved a measure directing city employees not to cooperate in federal criminal investigations in certain circumstances. Such efforts are largely based on misinformation and threaten to place the community at greater risk.

Both Democrats and Republicans in Congress came together to pass the Patriot Act: The House of Representatives voted 357 to 66 to approve it, and the Senate approved the legislation by a near-unanimous 98-to-1 vote. From my city and state, Rep. Nancy Pelosi and Senators Barbara Boxer and Dianne Feinstein, all Democrats, voted for the Patriot Act.

A Key Tool

While the Patriot Act is a key tool in the fight against terrorism, it provided for only modest, incremental changes in the law. The Patriot Act simply took existing legal principles and retrofitted them for the challenges posed by a well-financed and highly coordinated global terrorist network:

- First, the Patriot Act ensured that investigators could use the same tools in terrorism cases that have been available for many years in drug, fraud and racketeering cases. As Democratic Sen. Joe Biden of Delaware explained during the floor debate prior to passage of the act, "the FBI could get a wiretap to investigate the Mafia, but they could not get one to investigate terrorists. To put it bluntly, that was crazy! What's good for the mob should be good for terrorists."

- Second, the Patriot Act also brought the law up to date with current technology, so we no longer have to fight a digital-age battle with antique weapons from an era of rotary telephones.
- Third, the Patriot Act allows information-sharing and co-operation among government agencies so that they can better "connect the dots." The act recognizes that every level of law enforcement and first responders need to co-operate, contribute and share information to deal with the threats we face.
- Fourth, the Patriot Act increased the penalties for those who commit terrorist crimes so that we can take terrorists off the street and out of our communities.

Misinformation About the Patriot Act

Critics of the Patriot Act have created numerous myths about the act that have no basis in either the text of the law or in law-enforcement practice. For example, critics have charged that the FBI is unlawfully visiting local libraries to monitor the reading records of ordinary citizens. The fact is: business records, including library records, have been available to law enforcement for decades through grand jury investigations. (In the investigation of the Zodiac killer, for instance, police suspected that the murderer was inspired by a Scottish occult poet and wanted to learn who had checked the poet's books out of the library.)

> *Critics of the Patriot Act have created numerous myths about the act that have no basis in either the text of the law or in law-enforcement practice.*

The Patriot Act does not allow federal law enforcement free and unchecked access to libraries, bookstores or other businesses. The act only allows a high-ranking FBI official to ask a federal court to grant an order in specific investigations to "protect against international terrorism or clandestine intelligence activities." As a safeguard of our liberties, the act expressly bars the FBI from investigating citizens solely based on the exercise of their 1st Amendment rights.

Critics have also claimed that the Patriot Act encourages law enforcement to employ racial profiling and targeting. In fact, the act contains a provision explicitly condemning discrimination against Arab and Muslim Americans. The policy of the Justice Department is that terrorism investigations are to be governed by the principle of neutrality. We target criminal conduct, not nationality. . . .

As an immigrant to this country, I fully appreciate the unique constitutional rights that America offers her citizens. To this end, I will not tolerate the abuse of anyone's rights by law enforcement, nor will I accept anything less than the highest standard of ethical conduct by the prosecutors in my office. The protection of all our citizens' rights and privacy is the principle that guides us; failure to do so renders our efforts meaningless.

The Patriot Act, however, provides important tools that law enforcement can and should employ to fight the war on terror. I will not shrink from my sworn duty to do everything I can within the law to protect my district from terrorist attacks. Peoples' lives may well be at stake.

7

The United States Should Participate in the International Criminal Court

Human Rights First

Formerly known as the Lawyers' Committee for Human Rights, Human Rights First is a nonprofit advocacy organization that promotes human rights worldwide.

In 2002 the United Nations ratified the International Criminal Court (ICC) treaty, creating a permanent international court to prosecute war crimes and other human rights violations. Although 120 nations ratified the ICC treaty, the United States joined with only 6 other nations—most of them well-known human rights abusers—in opposing it. U.S. critics contend that the ICC may subject Americans overseas to unfair and politically motivated trials, but the ICC's civil rights standards are among the world's highest and the judicial independence of the ICC's diverse judges ensure that only legitimate cases will be pursued. The United States should join with its allies in supporting the ICC, thereby lending it greater credibility and increasing its effectiveness in dealing with rogue nations.

After repeatedly expressing support for establishing a permanent court to try those responsible for the worst international crimes, the United States voted against the adoption of the Rome Statute of the International Criminal Court (ICC) at the close of the Rome Diplomatic Conference on July 17, 1998.

The United States had participated actively in the Rome Conference, contributing most notably to the protections for due process and rights of the accused. But in the end it joined six others—including China, Iraq, and Sudan—in an attempt to defeat the establishment of the Court. These countries were in a minority: 120 nations, including all of the U.S.'s leading allies, voted in favor of the Court.

The concerns of the United States government focus on three key points. Each point has a basis in fact, but upon closer examination, reveals serious flaws.

1. The International Criminal Court will not become a forum for politically motivated Investigations and prosecutions of American citizens.

With the establishment of the International Criminal Court, some in the U.S. have expressed concern that this new international forum could be abused by anti-American powers for political purposes.

[Former Yugoslavian] President Slobodan Milosevic's petition to the International Court of Justice during the Kosovo air campaign, and Belgrade show trials of NATO [North Atlantic Treaty Organization] leaders prior to the Yugoslav presidential elections, are evidence of how governments hostile to the U.S. may attempt to use domestic and international legal mechanisms to embarrass the United States government and military.

> *Operating outside of any domestic political setting , . . . the ICC is less susceptible to political pressure than individual countries.*

The International Criminal Court, however, is likely to be a more reliable and credible judicial body than the national courts of many countries. The qualifications of the officials of the Court, including the judges and the Prosecutor, are measured by the highest standards. Operating outside of any domestic political setting, and staffed by international personnel representing a greater diversity of voices than is to be found in any single legal system, the ICC is less susceptible to political pressure than individual countries. Court officials are elected to nonrenewable terms by a majority of those countries that have ratified the ICC treaty (including all but one of the United States' NATO allies), and may be removed from office for specified misconduct by these same countries.

As lone voices in an international forum with defined processes, irresponsible states will not be able to monopolize this process, nor will the elected officials be held hostage by their political whims.

> *Americans need not fear the ICC any more than they need to fear American courts.*

The jurisdiction of the Court is circumscribed and subject to numerous safeguards. Countries are given ample opportunity to assert their right to try a case themselves. The Court may only investigate or prosecute a case if it finds that a country is unwilling or unable to do so itself. As a result, a judicial system as solid as the United States' will have primacy in all cases—even if officials decide the evidence does not warrant prosecution—provided the investigation or prosecution is genuine. In addition, the judges of the Court must endorse any decision of the ICC Prosecutor to initiate an investigation or prosecution, and countries can appeal the decisions of the Court. Furthermore, the United Nations Security Council has the authority to suspend an investigation or prosecution for renewable 12-month periods where the interests of peace and security so demand.

Should a case in fact go to trial before the International Criminal Court, the due process rights guaranteed by the ICC treaty (negotiated in no small part by the United States itself) ensure that proceedings will not be subject to political machinations. The rights accorded the accused are set out in greater detail than in any national judicial system, including that of the United States. In fact, the Rome Statute goes farther to safeguard constitutional protections than do many national courts to which the United States frequently extradites individuals.

Other countries with long-standing, fair, and reliable judicial systems have endorsed the ICC treaty, confident that the probability of political abuse is minimal. Americans need not fear the ICC any more than they need to fear American courts.

"The International Criminal Court will act only where national courts have failed to offer a remedy," said former British Foreign Secretary Robin Cook. "Therefore I think the concern about the U.S. Servicemen is misplaced. We in Britain would not be exposing our servicemen to vexatious prosecution. We have signed up to the International Criminal Court because we are confident there is no risk of that."

2. The International Criminal Court may prosecute Americans only if they are accused of a crime in a country that has ratified the ICC treaty and U.S. authorities do not genuinely Investigate the case.

In limited circumstances, the Rome Statute would allow the ICC to exercise jurisdiction over American citizens if they stand accused on reasonable grounds of committing crimes in countries that have ratified the ICC treaty. The United States argues that citizens of countries with solid judicial systems, such as the United States, should be shielded from the jurisdiction of the International Criminal Court, in particular when the suspects in question are acting in an official capacity (a defense argument that was rejected at the Nuremberg trials [of Nazi German war criminals]). The U.S. has gone so far as to suggest that countries do not have the right to delegate their national jurisdiction to an international court, and that all cases not involving citizens of countries that have ratified the ICC treaty should be tried only in national courts.

> *The International Criminal Court offers a highly respected and widely supported set of legal standards equal at least to those of the United States.*

The International Criminal Court was created by the nations of the world as an internationally sanctioned forum in which countries agree to try cases if their national courts are unable or unwilling to do so. If an American citizen commits a crime in a foreign country, whether in an official or unofficial capacity, basic international law already allows that country to try him or her. Similarly, that country may, by ratifying the ICC treaty, designate the International Criminal Court as a supplementary forum for trying the same case when it is unable or unwilling to do so itself. Of course, a nation's sovereign right to try those accused of committing crimes on their territory is always subject to their other international agreements and the law of immunities. The Rome Statute makes allowance for these.

> *The ICC does not impose new international law on U.S. military action.*

The International Criminal Court will always defer to national courts if they are willing and able to investigate or prosecute the crime. Since solid judicial systems are as a rule genuinely willing and able to do so, they need not fear that the ICC will inappropriately strip them of jurisdiction. The jurisdictional scope of the ICC may indeed restrict the ability of the United States to shield its citizens from foreign prosecution. But in the place of the current potential for any given nation to put an American citizen on trial, the International Criminal Court offers a highly respected and widely supported set of legal standards equal at least to those of the United States. The principle underlying the International Criminal Court is that no one, regardless of nationality, is beyond the rule of law.

3. The International Criminal Court will not unduly interfere with United States' ability to conduct overseas military operations.

United States armed forces engage in more military operations around the world than those of any other country, including a wide range of humanitarian and other interventions.

These operations are often highly complex and involve difficult judgment calls. In some situations, hundreds or even thousands of targeting decisions are made each day. An international court with jurisdiction over genocide, crimes against humanity, and in particular war crimes, is certain to remind anyone planning such complex military operations of the need to maintain vigilant adherence to the international laws of war. As a general rule, however, United States military personnel are not known to commit war crimes—much less genocide or crimes against humanity—particularly not with the intent and knowledge that are key elements of the ICC's definition of these crimes.

The ICC does not impose new international law on U.S.

military action. Each military targeting decision made by the U.S. armed forces is already subject to strict legal scrutiny by international lawyers in the employ of the U.S. military. Although U.S. law could be improved, existing procedures are broadly sufficient to meet the standards of the International Criminal Court.

The Court has no authority to determine whether or not a military operation can be conducted; it only has authority to adjudicate whether internationally recognized crimes are committed in the course of the operation. The knowledge that an independent, international body has the authority to adjudicate war crimes, crimes against humanity, and genocide certainly provides an added incentive for forces of all nations to act responsibly, an incentive clearly in the interest of the United States itself.

8

The United States Should Not Participate in the International Criminal Court

Gary Dempsey

Gary Dempsey is a foreign policy analyst for the Cato Institute, a libertarian public policy think tank. He is editor of the books Fool's Errands: America's Recent Encounters with Nation Building *(2001) and* Exiting the Balkan Thicket *(2002), and author of numerous articles on foreign policy.*

In 2002 the United Nations ratified the International Criminal Court (ICC) treaty, creating a permanent international court to prosecute war crimes and other human rights violations. The United States has opposed the ICC because the ICC does not contain the same level of civil rights guarantees provided for in the U.S. Constitution, which could subject U.S. military personnel to frivolous trials. Grounds for ICC trials sometimes include vague language, which can be broadly applied by courts at will. Furthermore, because the United States has more soldiers serving abroad than other countries, its military personnel will be disproportionately subject to ICC provisions. Under current provisions of the treaty, joining the ICC is not in the best interest of the United States.

The [President George W.] Bush administration opposes the creation of the ICC for a variety of sound reasons. But virtually every European leader backs the treaty, and the European press is howling that Washington's opposition is merely another example of American "unilateralism." According to diplomatic sources, Britain's foreign minister has even warned Secretary of State Colin Powell that the United States "does not want to be in a head-on clash with Europe" over the issue.

In truth, the transatlantic row over the ICC reveals far more about Europe's confusion than about America's motives.

Subordination of National Authority

For starters, the "unilateralism" slur arises from Europe's failure to distinguish between multilateral treaties and supranational treaties: Multilateral treaties rest on cooperation between independent nation-states pursuing overlapping interests. Supranational treaties seek to subordinate sovereign nation-states to new forms of international authority. The ICC falls in the latter category, and thus rejecting it is not really an example of "unilateralism," but a rejection of supranationalism.

European proponents of the ICC will scoff that the court is not meant to subordinate national courts and point to the treaty's preamble, which states that the court "is intended to be complementary to national criminal justice systems in cases where such trial procedures may not be available or may be ineffective." Trouble is, it's the ICC that ultimately gets to decide what constitutes an "effective" trial and has the last word on whether one must be made "available" in a given circumstance. The ICC, in other words, will have de facto supreme judicial oversight. So even when the court remains silent, it's making the final judgment.

> *American defendants brought before the ICC ... will not be accorded the rights guaranteed to them by the U.S. Constitution.*

American defendants brought before the ICC, moreover, will not be accorded the rights guaranteed to them by the U.S. Constitution—the right to a trial by jury, the right to confront witnesses against them, the right to compel witness in their favor, and the right against double jeopardy. The court's European proponents argue that this is not a problem because the United States already extradites American citizens to foreign countries where they are not guaranteed constitutional protections. But that misses the point: The U.S. government is not a party to the conduct and maintenance of foreign courts. If it ratifies the ICC treaty, however, the U.S. government would be a party to the conduct, maintenance, and indeed creation of a court that can try American citizens, which means their rights must be guaranteed or the court is unconstitutional.

> *The ICC treaty covers such vague offenses as causing 'serious injury to mental health' and committing 'outrages upon personal dignity.'*

The court's European cheerleaders counter that the constitutional question is unimportant because the ICC will be limited to only the most heinous crimes—war crimes, crimes against humanity, and genocide—so it's unlikely that even the most anti-American prosecutor will be in a position to haul Americans before the court. But to say "it will never happen" is a statement of faith, not law, especially because the ICC treaty covers such vague offenses as causing "serious injury to mental health" and committing "outrages upon personal dignity."

The Risk to U.S. Armed Forces

But the greater concern is that the court will expand its jurisdictional purview through an open-ended amendment process. Other crimes that already been suggested for the court include environmental crimes, cyber-crimes and drug trafficking. But the most likely first addition to the court's jurisdiction will be the crime of "aggression," which is already included in the treaty's text but is awaiting a formal definition. According to proposed wording, "aggression" could include such things as the "bombardment by the armed forces of a state against the territory of another state" and "the blockade of the ports or coasts of a state by the armed forces of another state." Including those actions under the rubric of "aggression" would sharply reduce the military options available to U.S. policymakers by outlawing preemptive strikes and the kind of naval blockade President John F. Kennedy employed during the Cuban Missile Crisis.

In an age when international terrorists are bent on acquiring weapons of mass destruction and targeting American civilians, ruling out preemptive strikes and blockades is suicidal. And ratifying the ICC treaty won't change the outcome much. The United States would have exactly as much say in the amendment process as other ratifying countries like San Marino and the Pacific atoll of Nauru.

What's more, the ICC treaty contains worrisome legal perversities. For example, a state that ratifies the treaty today can exempt itself from the jurisdiction of the court for seven years, but a country that doesn't ratify the treaty, for whatever reason, could have its citizens subjected to the court's jurisdiction as soon as it is created. In practical terms that means that signatory countries like Iran and Syria, which have been implicated in the use of torture and sponsoring terrorism against civilians, could have a free pass for the next seven years, but the United States, which is unlikely to ratify the treaty for constitutional and security reasons, could have its armed forces subjected to the ICC's scrutiny immediately. That is hardly an idle concern given that the United States is currently involved in hostilities overseas and has lately been the subject of near-hysterical European criticism over the detention of al Qaeda and Taliban fighters in [the U.S. military prison in] Guantanamo Bay, Cuba.

Finally, consider this: The United States currently maintains more than 200,000 soldiers and sailors outside its borders and has base rights in more than 40 countries. Because of that global presence the United States will automatically face far more exposure to the ICC's second-guessing than Europeans, who no one seriously expects to do any real fighting anytime soon. For that reason alone, European complaining should be ignored and the ICC treaty should be vigorously opposed.

9

Unregulated Globalization Threatens Human Rights

Alison Brysk

Alison Brysk is professor of political science and international studies at the University of California, Irvine. She is author of Globalization and Human Rights *(2002) and* Human Rights and Private Wrongs *(2005), as well as several other books and numerous articles on the topics of human rights, globalization, and international law.*

The term *globalization* refers to an increasingly global, cosmopolitan way of looking at the world—a point of view that impacts trade, foreign policy, and human rights. In some ways it is beneficial, building strong international coalitions and beneficial cultural exchanges. In other ways it is exploitative, allowing strong economic systems to easily dominate the weak and forcing distinctive cultures to conform to a generic and increasingly Western global standard. While it is not productive to speculate on whether globalization should be seen as a positive development—as it has both positive and negative consequences—the rights of individual human beings must be protected from the new dangers it presents. International regulation, enforced through the United Nations and bilateral treaties, is the best way to minimize the risk to human rights presented by globalization.

The odds are that it has touched you. Perhaps your immigrant family or neighbors came to this country seeking refuge from

Alison Brysk, "Globalization and Human Rights: It's a Small World After All," *Phi Kappa Phi Forum*, vol. 83, Fall 2003. Copyright © 2003 by Alison Brysk. Reproduced by permission of the publisher.

repression—or perhaps the shirt on your back was stitched by a virtual slave. It has certainly touched your wallet: your business, your pension fund, and your tax dollars may be bankrolling dictatorship or investing in freedom. And human rights have probably touched your conscience, when you read about mass graves with your morning coffee, answer an e-mail petition for women threatened with mutilation, or write a check for the latest victims of the latest war. Tens of thousands of Americans are risking their own lives in Bosnia, Afghanistan, Liberia, and Iraq, in part because we now believe (rightly or wrongly) that the atrocities of despotic regimes make our own world more dangerous. It's a small world after all—and often a very brutal and disturbing one.

The recognition of human rights and the weaving of a web of globalization are probably the most important political developments of our lifetimes. Like water carving a canyon, the slow, quiet power of human-rights pressures and aspirations helped bring down the Soviet empire, transform long-suffering Latin America, and construct unprecedented international institutions: the United Nations system. Meanwhile, the world is also more connected by trade, more susceptible to neighbors' weapons and distant wars, more bound together by the very vanishing air that we breathe—and the microbes it carries across borders. Globalization in all of these forms affects human-rights conditions for better and for worse, and at the same time, the spread of human rights ideals and institutions affects the shape of international integration. Understanding these connections is the key to building a small world worth living in.

The Impact of Globalization on Human Rights

Most lasting political change is driven by powerful ideas (good or bad), and the current era of globalization is no exception. These ideas inspire leaders, shape institutions, drive nations, and create communities—locally and globally. Ideas, in turn, evolve as they are adopted by new populations, tested in practice, and used to advance and resist the interests of the powerful.

Globalization and human rights both have roots in the powerful ideas of liberalism, which originated during the Enlightenment and evolved notably following the Second World War. The fundamental tenets of liberalism include the dignity of the individual, the desirability of freedom, the superiority of reason over belief, and the possibility of progress through exchange. By the end of the Cold War; most international interactions—from negotiations to lower tariffs to appeals against torture—shared the common elements of this world-view. But by the end of the twentieth century, the relationship between globalization and human rights had become more complicated—and at times, even contradictory.

> *❝ The recognition of human rights and the weaving of a web of globalization are probably the most important political developments of our lifetimes. ❞*

Human rights are universal principles affirming the inalienable dignity and equality of persons. The principle of human rights limits legitimate forms of coercion and deprivation that may be used in the exercise of authority, usually but not always by governments. . . . The "first generation" of rights inscribed in international treaties and institutions protects the individual's life, liberty, and bodily integrity from persecution and discrimination. A "second generation" of social and economic rights was introduced to international debate by developing countries and is gaining increasing recognition. For example, new trade agreements granting poor countries free access to patented pharmaceuticals seem to grant the legal basis for the "right to health" claimed by African AIDS patients. Finally, new challenges such as environmental devastation and new movements such as indigenous peoples' campaigns raise questions of a "third generation" of collective and cultural rights, which may be necessary to counter fundamental threats to survival and self-determination not captured by individual civil liberties. Human rights promise the first half of the liberal vision—freedom and the development of human potential through principle and law—but each of these kinds of rights is sometimes threatened by globalization's promise of progress through exchange.

Both promoters and protesters of globalization often equate globalization with trade; their debate centers on whether it means more Starbucks or more sweatshops. But globalization is actually an interconnected process of institutional, demographic, and cultural connection—not just economics. The desire for more Starbucks depends on cultural flows such as Hollywood images, and the customer base depends on social changes such as middle-class, high-tech incomes. Similarly, more sweat-shops also produce more migration, more transnational boycotts and organizations, and even more international law.

Although previous waves of globalization have occurred, the current era is distinguished by the strength and combination of four elements: connection, cosmopolitanism, communication, and commodification.

- Connection means greater traffic in bodies, goods, services, and information across borders.
- Cosmopolitanism describes the growth of multiple centers of power and influence above, below, and across national governments: international organizations, grassroots groups, and transnational bodies from Microsoft to Greenpeace.
- Communication is an increase in technological capacity that strengthens transnational networks of all kinds (from multinational corporations to nongovernmental organizations [NGOs] to terrorists) and diffuses ideas and values more quickly and broadly.
- Commodification is the expansion of world markets, and the extension of market-like behavior across more states and social realms. Increases in global capital flows, privatization of formerly state-owned enterprises, and increasing employment of children are all examples of commodification.

These disparate aspects of globalization help to explain why it is a double-edged sword for human rights. Connection brings human-rights monitors to Chiapas [Mexico, where police corruption and the use of torture are still common], but it also brings sex tourists to Thailand. Cosmopolitanism creates a UN Human Rights Commission and countless NGOs to condemn China's abuse of political dissidents and religious minorities; yet commodification makes China the United States's second-leading trade partner.

Although contradictory, these patterns are not random—research can map some factors that enhance or diminish globalization's impact on rights. First of all, we can distinguish the form of globalization. In general, interstate forms of international connection, such as conflict and migration, are threatening to human rights. But commodification and markets have a more mixed effect, sometimes providing employment and mobility but often fostering economic exploitation—which also may generate coercion and violence by businesses, smugglers, and corrupt governments. Overall, human rights are strengthened by the growth of cosmopolitan connections and global civil society, from international courts to transnational social movements. However, important exceptions to these trends exist.

Second, we must consider which kinds of rights are being affected. Civil rights are often enhanced by the connection, communication, and cosmopolitanism of globalization; the whole world is watching, and it will block your trade if you torture well-known political prisoners. But economic rights are often undermined by commodification and other forms of connection. Under pressure to service foreign debts, governments cut basic entitlements or ignore labor rights to attract foreign investors. The third generation of environmental and cultural rights is more episodic and usually depends on particular campaigns. Indigenous peoples are able to modify international dam projects that imperil their land, livelihoods, and cultures in Brazil, but not in China.

> **_Both promoters and protesters of globalization often equate globalization with trade. . . . But globalization is actually an interconnected process of institutional, demographic, and cultural connection—not just economics._**

Finally, globalization ironically increases the importance of the degree and direction of national governance. The same forces of commodification that subject Latin Americans to economic displacement, political chaos, and renewed repression are much less troublesome for a European, whose more developed government can buffer the shocks, negotiate effectively for citizens' interests in international institutions, and exercise social control without coercion. A Mexican peasant may lose her traditional land rights and government credits to a trade agreement concluded without her consent—then be beaten by the police when she protests. But a French farmer facing the same challenge has more leverage on his own government, basic welfare rights if things go wrong, reliable access to a range of speech and assembly rights to defend his interests, and appeal to the European Union for economic and civil-rights protection (and more subsidies). Further down the scale of national governance, the worst victims of globalization are people without any state protection: noncitizens, refugees, internally displaced persons, and women relegated to control of the "private authority" of family, community, or religion.

> ❝ Given a globalizing world and evolving threats to human dignity and survival, what can we do to change it? ❞

By combining these factors of the form of globalization, the type of rights affected, and the citizenship of the recipient, we can more accurately gauge the probable impact of globalization on rights. This more accurate picture should enable us to move beyond sterile debates on whether globalization is a good thing, without falling into a piecemeal case-by-case analysis. But the real question is, given a globalizing world and evolving threats to human dignity and survival, what can we do to change it?

The Human-Rights Response

Millions of human-rights activists around the world, and visionary leaders, have crafted a new way of doing politics to bring principle into practice. It begins by using global communications to capture the hearts and minds of global publics, who will pressure governments from the grassroots. Human-rights campaigns provide information on global suffering, affecting images that promote identification with victims and the formation of solidarity networks, and explanations that trace international connections. Advocates of human dignity must also construct cosmopolitan institutions at multiple levels, including global, regional, and sectoral organizations—from the International Criminal Court to the Organization of American States Human Rights Commission to the World Medical Association. And human-rights organizations actively promote the rule of national and international law. These strategies of mobilization and global governance can pressure governments [as political analyst Alison Brysk writes] "from above and below" to change repressive practices or better protect overlooked vulnerable citizens. But when the threat to human rights comes from global or private actors, human-rights proponents increasingly turn to an additional set of tactics. New forms of standard-setting, such as the Convention on the Rights of the Child, highlight new populations, construct new rights, inspire willing governments, and embarrass laggards. To enforce these standards on global and private actors, activists participate in global civic initiatives that bypass governments—such as codes of conduct for multinational corporations.

Most of the leading threats to human rights today reflect insufficient global governance. In the least-developed corners of the globe, pariah states and cultural relativists resist universal standards and international law—even as they seek global trade and security support. Furthermore, the crimes against humanity wrought by terrorist networks are more common and overall more costly in "failed" or weak states that lack both national and global governance. Terrorism flourishes in societies experiencing an unhealthy and unsustainable imbalance in these aspects of globalization.

> *Most of the leading threats to human rights today reflect insufficient global governance.*

At the other end of the spectrum, the [U.S. president George W.] Bush administration has sought to substitute American hegemony for global participation in a way that has damaged international human-rights treaties, programs, and institutions. For example, misguided U.S. objections and ultimate withdrawal from the International Criminal Court—which incorporated ample safeguards against political prosecutions—have complicated a goal that the United States claims to share: bringing war criminals and genocidal dictators to justice. Compounding this folly, U.S. policymakers have manipulated aid and trade agreements to impose special clauses exempting U.S. personnel from international legal accountability on states that had agreed to participate. U.S. rejection of international law also has diminished dominant power respect for human rights in the conduct of military interventions, the treatment of noncitizen immigrants, prisoners, and terrorism suspects, and even for the everyday civil liberties of U.S. citizens.

In a different way, the unbalanced commodification and

global-governance gap of neoliberal policies and pressures has generated impoverishment, destabilizing discontent, and decaying democracy in Latin America and parts of Africa and Asia. Powerful ideas have begun to receive policy feedback—showing that economic neoliberalism may contradict its namesake philosophy of liberalism, threatening human rights as it expands property rights. While the overall trend remains discouraging, human-rights resistance has already inspired some changes, such as debt relief. Continuing pressure may be building towards a chastened vision of a global safety net and rights consciousness for cosmopolitan economic institutions (both the World Bank and IMF [International Monetary Fund] now have human rights-related programs).

Human rights in the new millennium face a kind of "run on the bank," with expanding principles chasing too little authority. As with most global problems, the connection, communication, and resources exist to solve the problem—what is lacking is political will. Cosmopolitan institutions and rules can be strengthened at three levels. To strengthen global capacity, the United States must stop being the "deadbeat dad" of the UN and return to the family of nations. To bridge the gaps of chronically failing abusive governments, leading powers and regional organizations must build a systematic and humane system for multilateral humanitarian intervention—a kind of "governance of last resort." And the increasing influence of private actors—such as business or religious organizations—over the rights and conditions of millions requires a stronger set of global civic initiatives and monitoring, based in nonpartisan groups and affected sectors leveraging appropriate incentives such as investment.

In an era of globalization, defending human rights means more than the ongoing, still-necessary work of condemning distant dictators. It means tracing global connections, acknowledging global responsibilities, and rethinking national interest. In a small world, the rights you save may someday be your own.

10

Free Trade Promotes Human Rights

Daniel T. Griswold

Daniel T. Griswold is director of the Center for Trade Policy Studies at the Cato Institute, a libertarian public policy think tank. He is coeditor of Economic Casualties: How U.S. Foreign Policy Undermines Trade, Growth, and Liberty *(1999) and the author of numerous editorials and scholarly papers on issues pertaining to trade and immigration.*

The United States trades freely with some nations that have dismal records on human rights issues. Liberals and religious conservatives object to this practice because they say it provides encouragement and support to regimes that violate human rights. In truth, U.S. trade threatens such regimes by creating an empowered and financially successful class of citizens who are in a much better position to challenge a tyrannical government than a nation of impoverished serfs would be. A government that relies on international trade is much less likely to engage in war and gross human rights violations as they could disrupt trade and thereby threaten the national economy. The United States should continue to trade with tyrannical regimes not because it is efficient or morally acceptable, but because it is morally good. Free trade is one of the most effective ways to empower the oppressed and threaten their oppressors.

U.S. trade policy is almost always debated in terms of economic utility: Does free trade raise or lower incomes? Does it help or hurt U.S. industry? Does it create or destroy jobs? But behind the statistics and anecdotes lie moral assumptions about human nature, the sovereignty of the individual, and the role of government in a free society. Free trade may deliver the goods and boost efficiency, but is it morally superior to protectionism?

At the Summit of the Americas meeting in Quebec in April [2001], anti-capitalist protesters answered with a loud no, condemning free trade as a tool of the rich that exploits the poor and undermines democracy. Some religious conservatives portray free trade as a tool of the devil. Reform Party presidential candidate Pat Buchanan, in his 1998 book *The Great Betrayal*, called the doctrine of free trade "a secularist faith . . . born of rebellion against church and crown." Gary Bauer, former head of the Family Research Council and another failed aspirant to the White House, compares American trade with China with appeasement of the Soviet Union.

> *Friends of free trade should not shrink from making moral arguments for their cause; those arguments have deep roots in our culture.*

In a speech in May before the Council of the Americas, President [George W.] Bush joined the moral debate, telling his audience: "Open trade is not just an economic opportunity, it is a moral imperative. Trade creates jobs for the unemployed. When we negotiate for open markets, we are providing new hope for the world's poor. And when we promote open trade, we are promoting political freedom. Societies that open to commerce across their borders will open to democracy within their borders, not always immediately, and not always smoothly, but in good time."

The Moral Tradition of Free Trade

Friends of free trade should not shrink from making moral arguments for their cause; those arguments have deep roots in our culture. The Greek poet Homer, in his *Odyssey*, waxed poetic about the influence of trade:

> For the Cyclops have no ships with
> crimson prows,

no shipwrights there to build them
  good trim craft
that could sail them out to foreign
  ports of call
as most men risk the seas to trade
  with other men.
Such artisans would have made
  this island too a decent place to
  live in. . . .

The Judeo-Christian Bible warns against the pride that can come with riches, but it does not condemn international trade per se. In First Kings, it reports matter of factly that trade was part of King Solomon's splendor: "The king had a fleet of trading ships at sea along with the ships of Hiram. Once every three years it returned, carrying gold, silver and ivory, and apes and baboons." In the New Testament, in the second chapter of Matthew, we read about the famous wise men of the East, who traveled from Arabia or perhaps as far away as Persia to bring gold, frankincense, and myrrh to the baby Jesus. (Thank goodness they didn't have to contend with airport customs or the Arab boycott of Israel.)

> *There is no compelling moral reason why a small group of politicians should decide, on the sole basis of where things are produced, what goods and services an individual can buy with his earnings.*

The Old Testament prophet Ezekiel does warn the citizens of Tyre, the bustling Mediterranean port city, "By your great skill in trading you have increased your wealth, and because of your wealth your heart has grown proud." But even when the Bible speaks harshly of the "merchants of the earth," it is not international trade itself that comes under condemnation but the intent and character of the traders. The sin is not trade but dishonest scales, greed, indulgence in luxuries, and the temptation to pride that can come from wealth. In this respect, trade is no more sinful than technological discoveries or hard work.

A number of theologians and philosophers in the first several centuries A.D. considered trade among nations a gift of God. In his 1996 book, *Against the Tide: An Intellectual History of Free Trade*, Professor Douglas Irwin of Dartmouth College describes this early view of trade that has come to be called the Doctrine of Universal Economy. That doctrine held that God had spread resources and goods unevenly throughout the world to promote commerce between different nations and regions. . . .

Western moral thought provides a solid foundation for pursuing a policy of economic openness. Drawing on that tradition, here are seven moral arguments to support free trade among nations.

One: Free Trade Respects Individual Dignity and Sovereignty

A man or woman engaged in honest work has a basic right to enjoy the fruits of his or her labor. It is a violation of my right to property for the government to forbid me to exchange what I produce for something produced by a fellow human being, whether the person I'm trading with lives across town or across the ocean.

Protectionism is a form of stealing, a violation of the Eighth Commandment and other prohibitions against theft. It takes from one group of people, usually a broad cross section of consumers, and gives the spoils to a small group of producers whose only claim to the money is that they would be worse off under open competition.

> *There is no inherent conflict between good business and good morals, and in a free and open market under the rule of law the two complement each other.*

Free trade meets the most elementary test of justice, giving to each person sovereign control over that which is his own. As [economist] Frederic Bastiat wrote in his 1849 essay, "Protectionism and Communism":

> Every citizen who has produced or acquired a product should have the option of applying it immedi-

ately to his own use or of transferring it to whoever on the face of the earth agrees to give him in exchange the object of his desires. To deprive him of this option when he has committed no act contrary to public order and good morals, and solely to satisfy the convenience of another citizen, is to legitimize an act of plunder and to violate the law of justice.

Two: Free Trade Restrains the Power of the State

Free trade is morally superior to protectionism because it places trust in what [economic philosopher] Adam Smith called "the natural system of liberty" rather than in a man-centered system of centralized industrial policy. And by doing so it allows citizens to fulfill their creative and productive potential.

There is no compelling moral reason why a small group of politicians should decide, on the sole basis of where things are produced, what goods and services an individual can buy with his earnings. By diffusing economic decisionmaking as broadly as possible, free trade reduces the power of people in high places—always fallible and subject to temptation and abuse of power—to inflict damage on society.

As economists have been pointing out for two centuries now, the gains that protectionism confers on a select group of producers and the government's coffers are almost always outweighed by the losses imposed on the mass of consumers. This dead-weight loss weakens the productive capacity of a country as a whole compared to what it would be if its citizens were allowed to engage in free trade.

Producers who seek protection are not only robbing their fellow citizens of income and freedom of choice; they are sapping the economic strength of their own society. Protectionists are prone to wrap their agenda in words of patriotism and compassion, but their aim is self-centered and self-serving.

Three: Free Trade Encourages Individuals to Cultivate Moral Virtues

To be successful in a free and open marketplace, producers must serve their fellow human beings by providing goods and services others want and need. And the most economically successful will be those who provide not just for a select few but for a broad segment of consumers.

In the 1991 papal encyclical *Centesimus Annus*, Pope John Paul II observed that a market system encourages the important virtues of "diligence, industriousness, prudence in undertaking reasonable risks, reliability and fidelity in interpersonal relationships, as well as courage in carrying out decisions which are difficult and painful but necessary." On addition to such character traits, trade encourages good manners and the decent treatment of others.

> *By raising the general standard of living, free trade helps people to achieve higher levels of education and to gain access to alternative sources of information.*

In the long run, trade rewards those participants who act in a trustworthy manner. A supplier who misses deadlines for shipment or a buyer whose credit is no good will soon lose business to competitors with better reputations. In other words, there is no inherent conflict between good business and good morals, and in a free and open market under the rule of law the two complement each other.

Four: Free Trade Brings People Together

Trade opens the door for relationships that transcend economic exchange. When nations trade with one another, more than material goods crosses borders. People and ideas inevitably follow through the same open doors. Fax machines, cellular telephones, and the Internet are rapidly spreading as tools of international business, but they are also tools of friendship and evangelism.

At a Cato Policy Forum in 1999, Ned Graham, son of Billy Graham and president of East Gates International, spoke about the impact of expanding trade on his organization's missionary work in China:

> Ten years ago, there was almost no information-exchange technology available to the average Chinese citizen. If we wanted to contact a friend in

China, we usually had to do so by mail unless that individual had a private phone, which was extremely rare in the inland provinces. . . . Today, despite difficulties, much of that has changed. We routinely communicate with thousands of friends all over China via fax, cell phones, and email. The proliferation of information technology has allowed us to be much more effective in developing and organizing our work in the PRC [People's Republic of China].

Today more than 100 Western missionary groups are either working or attempting to work openly in China to spread the faith. Since 1992 Ned Graham's organization has legally distributed more than 2.5 million Bibles to nonregistered believers in China. This ministry would have been impossible without China's economic opening to the world that began 20 years ago and America's ongoing policy response of engagement. More than 20 million Chinese are now on the Internet, and that number has been growing exponentially. The number of telephone lines and cell phones in China has grown more than tenfold in the last decade. The works of Friedrich Hayek, probably this century's most influential defender of a free society, are now being distributed legally on the mainland. Free trade has brought new ideas and new relationships to China and other previously closed societies.

Five: Free Trade Encourages
Other Basic Human Rights

This is probably the most contentious of the seven reasons, and it goes to the heart of the current debate about trade with China and the use of sanctions in the name of human rights and democracy. By raising the general standard of living, free trade helps people to achieve higher levels of education and to gain access to alternative sources of information. It helps to create a more independent minded middle class that can form the backbone of more representative kinds of government. The wealth created from expanded trade can help to nurture and sustain civil institutions that can offer ideas and influence outside of government. The emergence of civil liberties and more representative government in countries such as Taiwan, South Korea, and Mexico can be credited in large part to economic development spurred by free trade and market reforms.

As a general rule, nations that are more open economically tend to enjoy other liberties as well. In the last 25 years, as the world has turned away from centralized economic controls and toward a more open global market, political and civil freedoms have also spread. In 1975 the nonprofit group Freedom House classified only 42 countries as politically free, meaning that citizens enjoy full civil and political freedoms. Today the number has more than doubled to 85. The percentage of the world's people enjoying full civil and political freedom has also more than doubled during that time, from 18 percent to 40 percent.

> *Religiously motivated conservatives who want to repeal normal trade relations with China would undermine progress on human rights by removing one of the most positive influences in Chinese society.*

In his book, *Business as a Calling*, [philosopher] Michael Novak explains the linkage with what he calls "the wedge theory":

> Capitalist practices, runs the theory, bring contact with the ideas and practices of the free societies, generate the economic growth that gives political confidence to a rising middle class, and raise up successful business leaders who come to represent a political alternative to military or party leaders. In short, capitalist firms wedge a democratic camel's nose under the authoritarian tent.

Religiously motivated conservatives who want to repeal normal trade relations with China would undermine progress on human rights by removing one of the most positive influences in Chinese society. Granted, the Chinese government today remains an oppressive dictatorship, a bad regime that jails its political opponents and interferes in the private lives of citizens. But for all its unforgivable faults, the Chinese government today is not nearly as bad as the government was during the totalitarian rule of Mao Tse-tung, when millions were killed and the entire social order was convulsed by the Great Leap Forward and the Cultural Revolution. The people of China do not yet enjoy the range of political and civil rights we do in the West, but they are freer and materially better off than they were three decades ago. For that they can thank economic and trade liberalization.

Six: Free Trade Fosters Peace

In an 1845 speech in the British House of Commons, Richard Cobden called free trade "that advance which is calculated to knit nations more together in the bonds of peace by means of commercial intercourse." Free trade does not guarantee peace, but it does strengthen peace by raising the cost of war to governments and citizens. As nations become more integrated through expanding markets, they have more to lose should trade be disrupted.

In recent years, the twin trends of globalization and democratization have produced their own "peace dividend": since 1987 real spending on armaments throughout the world has dropped by more than one-third. Since the end of the Cold War, the threat of major international wars has receded. In fact, today, virtually every armed conflict in the world is not between nations but within nations.

During the 1930s the industrialized nations waged trade wars against each other. They raised tariffs and imposed quotas in order to protect domestic industry. The result, however, was that other nations raised their barriers even further, choking off global trade and deepening and prolonging the global economic depression. Those dark economic times contributed to the conflict that became World War II. America's postwar policy of encouraging free trade through multilateral trade agreements was aimed at promoting peace as much as prosperity.

Seven: Free Trade Feeds and Clothes the Poor

Free trade and free markets empower poor people by giving them greater opportunity to create wealth and support their families. By dispersing economic power more widely, free trade and free markets undercut the ability of elites in less-developed countries to pillage a nation's resources at the expense of its poor. Proof can be found in the immigration patterns of poor people throughout the world. By the millions, they seek to leave closed and centrally controlled economies for those that are more open and less controlled. Poor people themselves understand that a free economy serves their interests, even if many of their self-appointed intellectual advocates in the West do not.

Nations open to trade tend to be more prosperous, just as cities along coastlines and navigable rivers tend to be wealthier than those in more remote, inland locations. The most recent *Economic Freedom of the World* study, by James Gwartney and Robert Lawson, found that the nations that were most open economically from 1980 through 1998 grew nearly five times faster than those that were most closed. And that trade-related growth lifts the lot of the poor. To cite the most dramatic example of this, the World Bank estimates that the number of Chinese citizens living in absolute poverty—that is, on less than $1 per day—has fallen since 1978 by 200 million. Revoking China's normal trade status, among all its other negative consequences, would set back one of the most successful anti-poverty programs in the history of mankind. In contrast, those regions of the world where poverty has been the most intractable, sub-Saharan Africa and South Asia, have been the least open to trade and foreign investment.

> *Free trade does not guarantee peace, but it does strengthen peace by raising the cost of war to governments and citizens.*

For all those reasons, trade sanctions fall heaviest on the poor of the target nation. Political rulers have the power to protect their pampered lifestyles, while the poor are left to suffer the consequences of U.S. policies that were enacted in the name of helping the very people they victimize. You can be sure that the communist leaders in Cuba and the ruling junta in Burma will continue to enjoy their fine, catered meals and chauffeur-driven cars while the millions of poor people they oppress are made even more miserable by U.S. trade and investment sanctions.

When all of the arguments are weighed, it should become clear that a policy of free trade is moral as well as efficient. Free trade limits the power of the state and enhances the freedom, autonomy, and self-responsibility of the individual. It promotes virtuous and responsible personal behavior. It brings people together in "communities of work" that cross borders and cultures. It opens the door for ideas and evangelism. It undermines the authority of dictators by expanding the freedom, opportunity, and independence of the people they try to control. It promotes peace among nations. It helps the poor to feed and care for themselves and creates a better future for their children. For which of these virtues should we reject free trade?

11

The United Nations Is Essential to Protecting Human Rights

Mary Robinson

Mary Robinson is director of the Ethical Globalization Initiative (EGI), an international human rights advocacy group. She served as president of Ireland from 1990 to 1997 and as UN high commissioner for human rights from 1997 to 2002.

The concept of human rights is not one that is universally understood. It is only through mutual agreement that it becomes an enforceable concept; before a government can address its complicity in violating human rights, it must first acknowledge that the rights actually exist. Essential to this role is the United Nations, which has proposed seven major human rights resolutions. The strength of these resolutions lies not in any direct power from the United Nations but rather in the power they give to diplomats and activists, who can cite these resolutions when protesting human rights violations. These resolutions collectively affirm that human rights include the rights to free speech, freedom of religion, and due process in criminal cases—but they also affirm the right to food and water, reasonable personal safety, health care, and other essential quality of life concerns. By linking all of these rights under the auspices of the international community, the United Nations can lead the world in improving the lives of the poor, marginalized, and oppressed throughout the world.

Mary Robinson, "Political Science and Human Rights: Tackling Global Inequalities," American Political Science Association, 100th Annual Meeting, September 4, 2004. Copyright © 2004 by Mary Robinson. Reproduced by permission.

As a member of the Helsinki Group on Globalization and Democracy, I was in Tanzania . . . when President [Benjamin] Mkapa of Tanzania, who was co-chair of the World Commission, made a passionate plea to us:

> I urge you to take up the challenge to agitate for the political will, in all governments, to do much more to improve the global governance of globalization, and to create opportunities for people within countries and opportunities for countries within the international system, to benefit more from globalization.
>
> Political and government leaders are beginning to understand that global peace and security cannot be guaranteed without global social and economic justice, and success in the war on poverty. The imbalances of power and influence, in the process, and the inequalities of the benefits of globalization, are not only a moral wrong; they are one of the factors fanning the flame of crime, nationally and across borders, and probably the ogre of terrorism. In an increasingly integrated world, it is futile for rich countries to believe they can shield themselves away from these negative aspects of globalization. It is in everyone's long term interest that these aspects are adequately addressed rather than wished away.
>
> For global governance to be fair, globalization must be much more inclusive than it is today. Democracy and human rights that are rightly demanded at the national level must be reflected at the global level. Otherwise, most of the developing countries will see calls of more democracy and human rights at the national level as hypocrisy and double standards.
>
> Globalization, and its governance, must be more inclusive politically, it must be more inclusive economically, and it must be more inclusive culturally. It must also be more inclusive in its promotion of human and social security. . . .

Statistics give us the numbers we account for in addressing inequalities, but they fail to convey the humiliation, the insecurities, the hopelessness, the lack of dignity involved. Listening to a family living in absolute poverty it is this lack they speak of: the lack of self respect, the indignity and humiliation of a refugee camp, the invisibility of being homeless, the helplessness in the face of violence, including violence caused by those in uniform who should protect.

And yet, starting with the [UN] Universal Declaration of Human Rights in 1948, and carried forward in the body of international law that has been painstakingly developed over half a century, the world has expressed through human rights a legal framework of shared commitment to the values of dignity, equality, and human security for all people. Our challenge . . . is to give those values practical effect both in our own communities and in the global community of nations. We each have a responsibility to help realize the vision of the Universal Declaration, in Eleanor Roosevelt's words, to make human rights matter "in small places, close to home."

> *Statistics give us the numbers we account for in addressing inequalities, but they fail to convey the humiliation, the insecurities, the hopelessness, the lack of dignity involved.*

I am very conscious, from speaking to public audiences, that almost everybody hears the words "human rights" differently. In the sense in which I refer to them here, human rights are legal tools for civil society groups to hold their governments accountable under the international human rights system. Every country in the world has ratified at least one of the core international human rights instruments [provided by the United Nations], of which there are seven. Let me list them, with the number of governments which have ratified them, to illustrate my point:

- The International Covenant of Civil and Political Rights, ratified by 152 countries
- The International Covenant on Economic, Social and Cultural Rights, ratified by 149 countries
- The Convention for the Elimination of Racial Discrimination, ratified by 169 countries
- The Convention Against Torture, ratified by 136 countries

- The Convention on the Elimination of Discrimination against Women, ratified by 177 countries
- The Convention of the Rights of the Child, ratified by 192 countries
- The Convention for the Protection of Migrant Workers and Their Families, ratified by 27 countries

Listing those government commitments leads me to a theme that was constant for me while UN High Commissioner for Human Rights and which remains such in my current work. Simply described, it concerns implementation and delivery. How do we move on from proclaiming the rights of people, and the obligations those rights give rise to on the part of states and the international community, towards the realization of those rights and obligations in practice, on the ground? How do we convert the great steps that have been taken to date, both to define rights and commit states to those definitions, into truly effective collective action at national and international levels to secure those rights for everyone in our world, without distinction? . . .

Human Rights and Human Security

Under the banner "all human rights for all," the Vienna World Conference on Human Rights in 1993 endorsed the strong link between human rights, democracy and development.

We began the 21st century with an important affirmation of that link. In September 2000, in New York, the largest gathering ever of heads of state and government expressed, through the United Nations Millennium Declaration, the international community's renewed commitment to the principles of justice and international law.

The Millennium Declaration stressed the need for sustained efforts to create a shared future, based upon our common humanity in all its diversity. It identified as the priority: "to make globalization work for all the world's people." The moment was marked by a spirit of re-dedication to international law and institutions as the best hope for the 21st century, and the Millennium Development Goals (MDGs) were agreed to, with specific targets and timelines, as the practical global agenda. These eight goals . . . include: halving those in extreme poverty and hunger by 2015; achieving universal primary education for boys and girls by 2015; and specific targets for promoting gender equality and empowerment of women; reducing child mortality; improving maternal health; combating HIV/AIDS, malaria and other diseases; ensuring environmental sustainability and developing a global partnership for development.

But just one year and three days after this historic declaration was adopted, the terrible events of September 11, 2001 [in which terrorists hijacked airliners and rammed them into the World Trade Center and the Pentagon] set the world on a different and much less hopeful course. Since that day, the commitments which ushered in the new century have been increasingly overshadowed by the threats of terrorism, by fears and uncertainties about the future, and by questions about the viability of open societies joined by international norms and values. The war in Iraq has been the most recent and extreme test to date of the international system's legitimacy and relevance in this new global environment.

Our post 9/11 world is preoccupied with different experiences of insecurity. The atrocities in Darfur, Sudan, the misery of the millions living with, and orphaned by, HIV and AIDS in sub-Saharan Africa, Asia and elsewhere, the long hardships suffered by indigenous peoples in the Americas, the humiliating poverty in slums and rural areas in the developing world—they all tell us a deplorable truth: that governments in different regions of the world are failing to provide even the rudiments of human security.

> *Starting with the [UN] Universal Declaration of Human Rights in 1948 . . . the world has expressed through human rights a legal framework of shared commitment to the values of dignity, equality, and human security for all people.*

In the United States and Europe the focus is on state security and combating acts of terrorism. But the stark reality is that the terrible attacks of 9/11 had no discernable impact on the millions of people already at daily risk from violence, disease and abject poverty. Their insecurity continues to stem from worry about where the next meal will come from, how to acquire medicines for a dying child, how to avoid the criminal with a gun, how to manage the household as a ten year old AIDS' orphan—the comprehensive insecurity of the powerless.

For women, gender is itself a risk factor threatening human security: the secret violence of household abuse, the private oppressions of lack of property or inheritance rights, the lifelong deprivations that go with lack of schooling and the structural problem of political exclusion.

Empowerment and Accountability

What I began to appreciate as President of Ireland—on visits, for example, to Somalia and Rwanda—and became convinced of during my five years in the UN—is that the underlying causes of practically all human insecurity are an absence of capacity to influence change at personal or community level, exclusion from voting or participating in any way in national decision making, and economic or social marginalization. The key to change lies in empowering people to secure their own lives. For this they need the means to try to hold their governments accountable, at local and national levels.

> *In the sense [used] here, human rights are legal tools for civil society groups to hold their governments accountable under the international human rights system.*

This broader understanding of human security was examined by an independent Commission on Human Security, co-chaired by Amartya Sen and Sadako Ogata. Their report, "Human Security Now" (2003), explains that human security involves a new paradigm which shifts from the security of the state to the security of the people—to human security. The emphasis is on the extent to which human security brings together the human elements of security, of rights and of development.

The report identifies two underlying concepts, protection and empowerment, which lie at the heart of human security. The first of these, protection, is primarily a state responsibility, and sometimes an international responsibility, as examined and clarified by the International Commission on Intervention and State Sovereignty in their report: "The Responsibility to Protect" (2001).

The Commission on Human Security describes the second

concept, empowerment, as: "People's ability to act on their own behalf—and on behalf of others . . . People empowered can demand respect for their dignity when it is violated. They can create new opportunities for work and address many problems locally. And they can mobilize for the security of others." This is a concept around which the human rights community and the political scientists' voice can join together and promote innovative examples. Essentially we need to make more visible, and build on, the grassroots movements which are challenging unfair global governance, and using the human rights framework to hold their governments more accountable for implementing rights to food, to safe water, to health and education, and for doing so without discrimination.

> *How do we move on from proclaiming the rights of people . . . towards the realization of those rights and obligations in practice, on the ground?*

I witnessed this grassroots work in every country I visited as High Commissioner. Human rights groups, women's groups, those working on child rights, with minorities, or tackling poverty were using tools of budget analysis and policy research to expose failures to implement progressively these rights, or to challenge expenditures on unnecessary military equipment or projects benefiting only a small elite. Invariably, the work was under-resourced, undervalued and often resented by those in power. Now these groups have additional tools available in the commitments both developed and developing countries have made to achieve the Millennium Development Goals by 2015, which will be reviewed during next year and debated at the [UN] General Assembly in September 2005. An opportunity presents itself, for political scientists among others, to reinforce the empowerment of grassroots organizations in every region, by helping them to link their country's undertaking to achieve the Millennium Development Goals, and the country's legal commitments to progressively implement economic and social rights under the relevant international treaties, together with developed countries commitment to substantial new resources for financing this development. . . .

The Role of the United States

There is a further link which needs to be made here in the United States. I have noted that when [U.S.] President [George W.] Bush emphasizes the importance of fighting terrorism and promoting freedom, he explains that it is not America's freedom he is referring to, but "Almighty God's freedom." I confess that I am troubled by this notion, and I prefer the approach which was advocated by President Mkapa of Tanzania in his speech: "To be the anchor of global peace and security, globalization must be promulgated by accepted universal values. But this imperative should not be translated as one set of countries imposing one set of values—whether political, economic, or cultural—on the rest of the world. Global values must be embedded in global dialogue, from best practices adapted to local conditions. We must all be contributory and determinative of the process towards the universal common good."

I would encourage you . . . to make it clear that freedom in this sense cannot be imposed and should encompass the broader idea of human security. In the words of Secretary General Kofi Annan: "Human security in its broadest sense embraces far more than the absence of violent conflict. It encompasses human rights, good governance, access to education and health care and ensuring that each individual has opportunities and choices to fulfill his or her own potential."

> **❝** In the United States and Europe the focus is on state security and combating acts of terrorism. But the stark reality is that the terrible attacks of 9/11 had no discernable impact on the millions of people already at daily risk from violence, disease and abject poverty. **❞**

Linking freedom and human security in this way could also have a positive impact on the allocation of resources. Additional money to support the Millennium Goals was pledged by the United States at a Conference on Financing for Development held in Monterrey, Mexico, through the Millennium Challenge Account. The European Union has also increased its commitment. However, there is still a wide disparity between the global spending on official development assistance, which amounts to around $60 billion a year, the annual amount developed countries spend on agricultural subsidies of $300 billion, and global military expenditure of $900 billion. It was estimated at Monterrey, by an eminent panel of economists chaired by Ernest Zedillo, that an additional $50–60 billion annually on development assistance would be needed to ensure full implementation of the Millennium Development Goals by 2015. If this extra expenditure would in fact make the world more secure, does it not seem like a good investment? . . .

> *The key to change lies in empowering people to secure their own lives. For this they need the means to try to hold their governments accountable, at local and national levels.*

The project I lead in New York, Realizing Rights: The Ethical Globalization Initiative [EGI], is seeking to extend a human rights analysis and strong gender perspective into issues of trade and development; into health issues—particularly the pandemic of HIV and AIDS in sub-Saharan Africa—and into migration. We want to build a bridge of shared language and understanding with other disciplines—with economists, development experts, social scientists and, of course, political scientists. We hope to be able, as a catalyst, to engage some leaders in government, in business, the trade union movement, the women's movement, and people of faith in thinking creatively about how—from different perspectives—we can create multi-stakeholder approaches to global problems and help empower grassroots and social movement groups. We believe this empowerment can be strengthened with knowledge of the additional tools by which to hold their governments accountable for both their human rights commitments and the implementation of the Millennium Development Goals with additional resources over the next ten years.

Let me conclude by highlighting the emphasis placed by Shirin Ebadi of Iran, the 2003 Nobel Peace Prize winner, on the universality of human rights. In her contribution to the "Human Development Report 2004," she begins by identifying the differences in people that are part of cultural diversity. She then emphasizes that human rights embody the fundamental values of human civilizations and concludes:

> "So cultural relativity should never be used as a pretext to violate human rights, since these rights embody the most fundamental values of human civilizations.

> The Universal Declaration of Human Rights is needed universally, applicable to both East and West. It is compatible with every faith and religion. Failing to respect our human rights only undermines our humanity.

> Let us not destroy this fundamental truth; if we do, the weak will have nowhere to turn."

12

The United Nations Does Not Respond Effectively to Human Rights Abuses

Mark Falcoff

Mark Falcoff is a resident scholar emeritus at the American Enterprise Institute, a moderately conservative public policy think tank. He also teaches at the University of Illinois and the University of California at Los Angeles. He has served as a staff member on the Senate Foreign Relations Committee, and he was a member of the 2003 U.S. delegation to the UN Human Rights Commission.

The United Nations attempts to address human rights violations through its Human Rights Commission (HRC). Unfortunately, this commission—recently chaired by Libya—is made up of some of the world's worst human rights offenders. Because of this, gross human rights violations such as mass executions and widespread suppression of free speech are swept under the rug in favor of discussions regarding the "right" to adequate housing, the "right" to proper toxic waste disposal, and other humanitarian issues that are not rights in the traditional sense of the word and do not challenge oppressive governments. The UN Human Rights Commission as it is presently constituted is seldom relevant to the concerns it was created to address.

Mark Falcoff, "Behind the Human Rights Mask," *The American Enterprise*, vol. 14, December 2003. Copyright © 2003 by the American Enterprise Institute for Public Policy Research. Reproduced by permission of *The American Enterprise*, a magazine of Politics, Business, and Culture. On the web at www.TAEmag.com.

Readers of *The American Enterprise* may have been a little surprised when the United Nations Human Rights Commission failed to pass a resolution condemning Cuba at its 59th annual session in Geneva [in] March and April [2003]. After all, the [Fidel] Castro dictatorship had arrested nearly 80 journalists, librarians, and human rights activists literally days before, and sentenced them behind closed doors to prison sentences as long as 25 years. When the U.N. Economic and Social Council meeting in New York a few days later actually voted to re-elect Cuba as a member of the Human Rights Commission [HRC], instead of the object of one of its investigations, any reasonable observer might have been strained.

Strange Membership

In my own case, however, the reaction to both events was somewhat muted. I knew what to expect—for I had been a member of the U.S. delegation to the U.N. Human Rights Commission's Geneva meetings. After that experience, nothing the U.N. does will be capable of shocking me.

> *The [U.N. Human Rights] Commission (like the U.N. itself) is home to some of the world's most unsavory regimes.*

In the first place, the Commission (like the U.N. itself) is home to some of the world's most unsavory regimes. No less than 53 countries are represented on the HRC. The membership was arrayed in concentric ovals in Geneva, and, amazingly, the inner oval consisted of outright police states: countries like Syria, Iran, Egypt, Saudi Arabia, Algeria, China, Vietnam, Zimbabwe, Cuba, and Colonel Qaddafi's Libya (which, almost amusingly, currently chairs the Human Rights Commission). The next oval outward grouped together countries slightly less objectionable but who often vote with the first group—India, Pakistan, most of the African countries, plus odd ducks like Colonel [Hugo] Chavez's Venezuela. The third oval is made up of most of the Latin American republics plus South Africa, and (on some issues) small European countries like Ireland or Belgium—who are currently trying out for the role of Progressive Conscience of Humanity. They sometimes vote with the Western democracies, but are generally unreliable. Both Argentina and Brazil abstained on this year's Cuban resolution—one that didn't even condemn the Castro regime but merely begged the dictator to allow a representative of the Commission in to "evaluate" the situation. South Africa likewise managed to kill a resolution on Zimbabwe because, whatever his sins, dictator Robert Mugabe is, after all, black. (So are his victims—a point Pretoria [the capital of South Africa] chooses to overlook.)

> *In U.N.-speak, the 'rights' that are regarded as fundamental are airy ones like the 'right' to food, the 'right' to adequate housing, the 'right' to clean air and clean water . . . and so forth.*

The fourth oval encompasses the only countries that have any right to be there at all the democracies built on genuine individual rights: the Western European countries, the United States, Canada, Australia, New Zealand, and Israel. These are in a distinct minority and have to do some powerful horse trading with the second and third ovals just to maintain a grasp on the agenda.

Five Criticisms of the U.N. Human Rights Commission

As long as the Commission is allowed to be this large, and refuses to impose any real-world tests for membership (does the country in question actually respect human rights itself?), it is simply naive to expect anything productive of this organization.

A second reason not to expect much of U.N. bodies like this is that in the world of the United Nations, what are called economic and social rights are supposedly given equal weight to civil and political rights (although in practice the latter are most often treated as an expensive luxury that nobody really needs). In U.N.-speak, the "rights" that are regarded as fundamental are airy ones like the "right" to food, the "right" to adequate housing, the "right" to clean air and clean water, the "right" to proper disposal of toxic wastes, and so forth. By clogging the agenda with such practical issues, the Third World countries deflect attention from their prisons and torture chambers. Their selective terminology allows them to sit in judgment on Western countries. After all, their constitutions declare the "right to food"—does yours?

> *[The] State Department is . . . apparently unfazed by [the countries that make up the] membership [of the Human Rights Commission], its leadership, [and] its failure to focus seriously on real human rights violations.*

Third, from the United Nations point of view, human rights are advanced only to the degree to which vast bureaucracies are created and expanded. If there is a problem, the U.N. proposes to create tax-free jobs for bureaucrats and politicians (mostly from undemocratic states), paid for largely by the "rich" countries. If you balk at this, that proves "you don't care about human rights." If you do pony up the cash, somehow human rights are being advanced—regardless of the actual situation on the ground.

Fourth, far too much time is devoted to letting the so-called Non-Governmental Organizations (NGOs) have their say. Most of these are not really non-governmental in any meaningful sense. Some, like the Federation of Cuban Women, are actually state propaganda organs. Others are financed by the U.N. or the European Union, or individual European governments. Many others are creatures of regional bodies like the Arab League. I would estimate that speechifying from such groups takes up roughly 35 to 40 percent of the time of U.N. agencies. This has concrete economic consequences, because the translators earn $300 an hour, and there are five official languages at the U.N., which means every speech has to be translated in 25 different directions. The United States pays for 23 percent of the costs of this. The length of the sessions—and the corresponding bill— could be drastically reduced by eliminating NGO pontificating, which adds nothing whatever to the deliberations.

Fifth and finally, it is distressing to see how deeply our own State Department is committed to quixotic ventures like the U.N. Human Rights Commission—apparently unfazed by its membership, its leadership, most of all, its failure to focus seriously on real human rights violations. Too many of our diplomats, like diplomats everywhere, seem to be fascinated by process. Some even seem distressingly anxious to win the approval of thugs and murderers. As one told me, "if there are 190 countries in the world and they all vote against you, maybe you're wrong." I found myself replying to him somewhat tartly that overwhelming sentiment can't change the facts of a matter.

I don't think I'll be invited back next year.

13

Democracy Promotes Human Rights

Natan Sharansky, with Ron Dermer

During the 1970s Anatoly Sharansky served as an interpreter for Andrei Sakharov, a Soviet physicist and nuclear disarmament activist who would later receive a Nobel Peace Prize for his work. Following Sakharov's house arrest, Sharansky was captured and imprisoned by the Soviet Union in 1978—both were punished for their beliefs. Sharansky was sent to Israel in 1986 as part of a prisoner exchange, at which time he adopted the traditional Jewish name of Natan and became active in Israeli politics. He currently serves on the cabinet of Israeli prime minister Ariel Sharon. He is author of two books: Fear No Evil *(1988), a memoir, and* The Case for Democracy *(2004), from which this article is excerpted. Ron Dermer is a former columnist for the* Jerusalem Post.

Human rights can only be reliably protected in democratic societies ("free societies") because it is only in democracies that the people of a country may hold their government directly accountable for its actions. Under totalitarian regimes ("fear societies"), human rights will inevitably be violated because fear and oppression are the means by which such governments control the people they rule. That peace activists and human rights organizations are more likely to criticize democracies such as the United States and Israel than they are to criticize nondemocratic governments reflects a profound lack of perspective. The struggle between democracy and totalitarianism is nothing less than a struggle between good and evil.

Natan Sharansky, with Ron Dermer, *The Case for Democracy: The Power of Freedom to Overcome Tyranny and Terror.* New York: PublicAffairs, 2004. Copyright © 2004 by Natan Sharansky and Ron Dermer. All rights reserved. Reproduced by permission of PublicAffairs, a member of Perseus Books LLC.

One way to see today's lack of moral clarity is to take note of the confusion that continues to surround the question of human rights. Rather than serve as a sacred principle that leaves little room for doubt, human rights have always been mired in controversy. When the Universal Declaration of Human Rights was drafted at the United Nations in 1948, it was adopted without dissent, but with abstentions by Soviet bloc nations, South Africa, and Saudi Arabia. As is true of any attempt to bridge the unbridgeable moral gap between dictatorship and democracy, the declaration stood for everything, and hence, for nothing.

This was good news for the Soviet Union, which always tried to undermine efforts to bring moral clarity to the issue of human rights. As Western leaders justly denounced the human rights record of the communist superpower, Soviet leaders consistently attacked liberal democracies in the language of human rights by wrapping them in the mantle of "social justice"—a social justice that was being used by those same regimes to justify the murder of tens of millions of their own subjects.

Freedom and Fear

Still, for those who were not totally blinded by the egalitarian newspeak of tyrants like [Soviet dictator Josef] Stalin, [Chinese leader] Mao [Tse-tung], and [Cambodian dictator] Pol Pot, the Cold War offered something of an antidote to the obfuscation of human rights issues. By splitting the world into two, the struggle between the totalitarian East and the democratic West helped clarify the conflict—at least for those willing to open their eyes—as a battle between good and evil, right and wrong.

For dissidents within the former Soviet Union, these moral lines were practically self-evident. Unlike philosophers and rights activists in the West, we dissidents did not feel the need to split hairs over the precise nature of human rights.

We knew that to determine whether or not human rights were being generally upheld in a particular country, we only had to ask a few simple questions:
- Could people in that country speak their minds?
- Could they publish their opinions?
- Could they practice their faith?
- Could they learn the history and culture of their people?

We understood that for those living in a fear society, the answer to most of our questions, if not all of them, was no. The structural elements that enable democratic societies to respect human rights—independent courts, the rule of law, a free press, a freely elected government, meaningful opposition parties, not to mention human rights organizations—were all glaringly absent in fear societies. While these structures are not always sufficient to ensure the protection of human rights, our experience had convinced us that without them, human rights would inevitably be crushed. Every political prisoner in the Gulag [Soviet prison] recognized the moral chasm that separated free societies and fear societies. We recognized that a free society did not guarantee the protection of human rights, but we knew that a fear society guaranteed their violation.

> *Rather than serve as a sacred principle that leaves little room for doubt, human rights have always been mired in controversy.*

Yet the connection between democracy and human rights that seemed so clear to us dissidents was often ignored in the West. The blindness to this connection by many of those whom we saw as natural allies in the human rights struggle was a source of constant disappointment for those fighting for freedom within the Soviet Union. We dissidents could ready ourselves psychologically for a life of risk, arrest, and imprisonment. But we could never fully prepare ourselves for the disappointment that came from seeing the free world abandon its own values. And nowhere was this disappointment more bitterly experienced than from the confines of a prison cell.

Religious Freedom in the USSR

An example was the trip of the world-famous evangelical preacher, Billy Graham, to the Soviet Union in 1984. For many years before and since, Graham and his followers have been a driving force for moral clarity in world affairs. But on this particular trip, Graham helped the cause of moral equivalence. When he arrived in the Baltic Republics, a region with a large number of Protestants, Graham was permitted to deliver his riveting sermons in packed stadiums. In an interview following one of those sermons, he was asked to describe freedom of religion within the Soviet Union. After remarking that he had been free to preach wherever he wanted, Graham observed that challenges relating to religious freedoms were not particular to the USSR. "You have some problems with religion," he told the Soviet journalist, and "the United States has problems with religion." Both countries, Graham said, could do better.

Sitting in my prison cell, I read about Graham's visit in *Pravda*, the government-controlled newspaper we were permitted to read. *Pravda*'s editors naturally gave pride of place to the American preacher's comments about freedom of religion inside the Soviet Union. I was dumbfounded. How could Graham possibly place religious freedom in a free society like the United States on a par with religious freedom in a fear society like the Soviet Union? Did the heated debates in America over the separation of church and state blind Graham to the fact that individuals in the USSR were completely denied the right to practice their faith? Did Graham not understand that he was giving legitimacy to a system that sought to eradicate religion completely?

Though Graham was free to preach to tens of thousands of people, my own cellmate, Vladimir Poresh, who was Greek Orthodox, was given a seven-year sentence for teaching Christian "propaganda" to fewer than ten people. Our fellow prisoners included many of Graham's fellow Pentecostals, who were first exiled to Siberia and later persecuted for trying to teach religion to their own children. . . .

> *The struggle between the totalitarian East and the democratic West helped clarify the conflict—at least for those willing to open their eyes—as a battle between good and evil, right and wrong.*

At least Graham later regretted his remarks. But the same cannot be said about the many peace activists in the early 1980s who showed a similar lapse of moral clarity. In response to the Soviet buildup of intermediate range nuclear missiles, President [Ronald] Reagan and Western European leaders were determined to deploy Pershing nuclear missiles in Europe to deter any possible Soviet attack on the Continent. Millions of people took to the streets in Western European capitals protesting that the real aggressors were the warmongering American president and his European allies, not the Soviets. The leaders of the anti-nuclear rallies pointed to the "peace activists" from the USSR who were denouncing Western aggression and marching alongside them as proof that the Soviets wanted peace. But those who were marching in Europe were a hand-picked delegation sent by the Soviet regime to increase pressure on Western governments to reverse their position and remove the Pershings. Meanwhile, the real peace activists in the USSR, those who had demanded that the Soviets disarm, were languishing in prison with me.

> // We recognized that a free society did not guarantee the protection of human rights, but we knew that a fear society guaranteed their violation. //

While Graham and the peace activists certainly did not intend to crush the spirits of dissidents inside the USSR, that was the effect of their actions. I am sure Iranians fighting for their freedom felt a similar dejection when an official in the American State Department recently referred to their country as a democracy. . . .

Unbalanced Criticism

When a human rights organization I deeply respected also chose to ignore the important moral distinction between free and fear societies, I realized the full extent of the problem. Amnesty International, an organization dedicated to fighting human rights abuses around the world, is well known for its support of prisoners of conscience and the right of dissent. I felt a strong personal connection to Amnesty International: Several of my friends were sentenced to prison for collecting information on its behalf, and I myself had been a beneficiary of their indefatigable efforts to raise awareness about political dissidents and to fight for their release. I thought of Amnesty as an organization with which I could completely identify.

Soon after I arrived in Israel, I met with Amnesty officials. It felt like a reunion of old comrades. I gave them information on other prisoners and the conditions of the camps in which I had stayed. They gave me a copy of their annual human rights report and told me about their ongoing campaigns for dissidents around the world. I was honored when they asked me to speak at a meeting later that year in London.

But when I began to flip through the pages of the annual report I immediately noticed that something was terribly wrong. There were pages and pages of material about human rights abuses in my new country, Israel, and very little on the non-democratic states that surrounded us. It appeared as though Israel was a bigger violator of human rights than Saudi Arabia, a country where there was no freedom of speech, no freedom of the press, and no freedom of religion. In fact, the impression one got from the report was that Israel was one of the worst human rights abusers in the world, if not the worst. When I was given the opportunity to speak to Amnesty supporters in London later that year, I decided to address the matter head on.

I pointed out that precisely because Israel is an open society where the press is free to criticize the government and where human rights organizations are free to issue damning reports, it is much easier to garner information on human rights abuses in Israel than in closed societies. While I told the audience that I did not believe human rights abuses in Israel should ever be glossed over or hidden from the public eye, I offered what I thought was a constructive suggestion. Why not divide the report into three sections, one for totalitarian regimes, one for authoritarian regimes, and one for democracies? Without those categories, Amnesty was creating a dangerous moral equivalence between countries where human rights are sometimes abused and countries where they are *always* abused.

> *How can a human rights organization be impartial about political systems that are inherently hostile to human rights?*

The reply of Amnesty officials following my speech was extremely disappointing. "We are not going to label countries," they told me. "We will simply show the picture as it is." Nearly twenty years later, Amnesty has not changed its policy. It continues to proudly state that it "does not support or oppose any political system" because it is "concerned solely with the impartial protection of human rights." But how can a human rights organization be impartial about political systems that are *inherently* hostile to human rights? No doubt, its dedicated activists believe that this impartiality between fear and free societies does not undermine the cause of human rights. But it does.

How Free Societies Respond to Human Rights Violations

In the post 9/11 world, many democratic governments now have a better appreciation of how difficult it can be to find the appropriate balance between providing maximum security to your citizens and protecting human rights. In debating issues like the Patriot Act [antiterror legislation passed in 2001] or the rights granted to prisoners at Guantanamo Bay [a U.S. military prison in Cuba], Americans are confronting a dilemma that Israel has faced since the day it was established.

> *Human rights violations can and do take place in democratic societies. But one of the things that set democracies apart from fear societies is the way they* respond *to those violations.*

Human rights violations can and do take place in democratic societies. But one of the things that sets democracies apart from fear societies is the way they *respond* to those violations. A fear society does not openly debate human rights issues. Its people do not protest. Its regime does not investigate. Its press does not expose. Its courts do not protect. In contrast, democratic societies are always engaged in self-examination.

For example, look at how the United States dealt with the [2003] abuse and humiliation of Iraqi prisoners by American soldiers in Abu Ghraib prison. Even before the abuse became publicly known, the army had suspended those involved and was conducting a full investigation. And as soon as the disturbing pictures of the abuse were published, America's democracy was shocked into action. The Congress, determined to find the culprits, immediately convened public hearings, and demanded a full account of what led to the abuse. Politicians and opinion makers insisted that the people responsible for the abuse be held accountable, including those at the very top of the chain of command. The media mulled over the details, pursuing every allegation, tracking down every lead. The American people openly discussed what the abuse said about their own country's values, its image in the world, and how that image would affect the broader War on Terror. The U.S. president, for his part, apologized to the families of the victims and said that those responsible would be punished.

But let's not forget that the treatment of prisoners at Abu Ghraib under [former Iraqi president] Saddam [Hussein] was far worse than anything America was accused of. Yet were pictures distributed of Saddam's soldiers murdering, raping, and torturing Iraqis? If they had been distributed, would Iraq's parliament have conducted public hearings? Would the Iraqi media have reported it? Would anyone have publicly called for the resignation of Saddam's defense minister, let alone Saddam himself? Would Saddam have denounced the brutality and apologized to the victims and their families?

Far from showing that all societies are the same, the human rights abuses that sometimes occur in democracies often help illustrate the tremendous moral divide that separates free and fear societies. While I have not always agreed with the decisions made by my government on issues related to human rights, my experience has made me confident that these issues are thoroughly discussed and debated and that the need to protect human rights is never ignored. I suspect that in most other free societies the situation is much the same. Every democratic state will choose its own balance between protecting security and protecting human rights, but concern for human rights will always be part of the decisionmaking process. The free world is not perfect, but the way it responds to its imperfections is only further proof that human rights can only be protected in democratic societies.

14

Illiberal Democracy Can Threaten Human Rights

Fareed Zakaria

Fareed Zakaria is editor of Newsweek International *and holds a PhD in international relations from Harvard University. He regularly appears on television news programs and is author of three books, including* The Future of Freedom *(2003), from which this article is excerpted.*

Conventional wisdom suggests that democracy leads to a liberal government that respects human rights, but this is not always the case. Sometimes democracy restricts human rights by putting popular dictators into power or by restricting the rights of minority groups through majority rule. This problem is particularly evident in Latin America and Central Asia. In a country where the majority of the population opposes policies friendly to human rights—as in Pakistan, for example—an unelected but reform-minded military dictator may be a much better hope for freedom than an elected leader.

During the last two decades in Africa and in parts of Asia and Latin America, dictatorships with little background in constitutional liberalism or capitalism have moved toward democracy. The results are not encouraging. In the Western Hemisphere, with elections having been held in every country except Cuba, a 1993 study by one of the leading scholars of democratization, Stanford's Larry Diamond, determined that ten of the twenty-two principal Latin American countries had "levels of human rights abuse that are incompatible with the consolida-

Fareed Zakaria, *The Future of Freedom: Illiberal Democracy at Home and Abroad.* New York: W.W. Norton & Company, 2003. Copyright © 2003 by W.W. Norton & Company, Inc. Reproduced by permission.

tion of [liberal] democracy." Since then, with a few important exceptions such as Brazil, things have only gotten worse.

Consider Venezuela's Hugo Chavez. A colonel in the army, he was cashiered and jailed for his part in an unsuccessful coup d'état in 1992. Six years later, running on an angry, populist platform, he was elected president with a solid 56 percent of the vote. He proposed a referendum that would replace Venezuela's constitution, eviscerate the powers of the legislature and the judiciary, and place governing authority under a "Constituent Assembly." The referendum passed with 92 percent of the vote. Three months later his party won 92 percent of the seats in the new assembly. The proposed new constitution increased the president's term by one year, allowed him to succeed himself, eliminated one chamber of the legislature, reduced civilian control of the military, expanded the government's role in the economy, and allowed the assembly to fire judges. "We are heading toward catastrophe," warned Jorge Olavarria, a longtime legislator and former Chavez supporter. "This constitution will set us back 100 years, and the military will become an armed wing of the political movement." The new constitution passed in December 1999 with 71 percent of the vote. Despite the fact that Venezuela went through grim economic times during his first few years, Chavez never dropped below 65 percent in public approval ratings.

By early 2002 it seemed as if his luck was finally running out. Public discontent with his thuggish rule and a failing economy combined to spark massive demonstrations. The army and business elites plotted a coup and, in March 2002, Chavez was ousted—for two days. Chavez, who is skilled at organizing "people power"—and who was helped by the blatantly undemocratic nature of the coup—was comfortably back in power within a week.

Broken Democracies

Venezuela has the telltale sign of democratic dysfunction: abundant natural resources, including the largest oil reserves outside the Middle East. This has meant economic mismanagement, political corruption, and institutional decay. Four out of five Venezuelans live below the poverty line in a country that, twenty years ago, had among the highest living standards in Latin America. In some ways the country was ripe for a revolution. But what it got was a new *caudillo* [military dictator], a strongman who claims to stand up for his country against the world (which usually means the United States). This is why Chavez has shown his admiration for Fidel Castro [of Cuba], Saddam Hussein [of Iraq], and even the loony Mu'ammar Gadhafi [of Libya]. More dangerously, Chavez represents a persistent hope in Latin America that constructive change will come not through a pluralist political system, in which an array of political parties and interests grind away at the tedious work of incremental reform, but in the form of some new, messianic leader who can sweep away the debris of the past and start anew. This tendency has been gaining ground throughout the Andean region in the last few years. If Latin America's economic woes persist, it could become more widespread.

> **❝** A 1993 study by one of the leading scholars of democratization . . . determined that ten of the twenty-two principal Latin American countries had 'levels of human rights abuse that are incompatible with the consolidation of [liberal] democracy. **❞**

In Africa the past decade has been a crushing disappointment. Since 1990, forty-two of the forty-eight countries of sub-Saharan Africa have held multiparty elections, ushering in the hope that Africa might finally move beyond its reputation for rapacious despots and rampant corruption. The *New York Times* [in 2002] compared this wave of elections to the transitions in eastern Europe after the fall of communism. This is a highly misleading analogy, however. Although democracy has in many ways opened up African politics and brought people liberty, it has also produced a degree of chaos and instability that has actually made corruption and lawlessness worse in many countries. One of Africa's most careful observers, Michael Chege, surveyed the wave of democratization in the 1990s and concluded that the continent had "overemphasized multiparty elections . . . and correspondingly neglected the basic tenets of liberal governance." These tenets will prove hard to come by, since most of Africa has not developed economically or constitutionally. It is surely not an accident that the two countries in Africa that are furthest along on the path toward liberal democracy, South Africa and Botswana, have per capita incomes above the zone of transition to democracy, which was from $3,000 to $6,000. South Africa's is $8,500 and Botswana's $6,600; both are artificially high because of natural-resource wealth. None of this is to say that Africa was better off under its plundering dictators, but it does suggest that what Africa needs more urgently than democracy is good governance. There are some extraordinary success stories, such as Mozambique, which ended a sixteen-year civil war and is now a functioning democracy with a market economy. But it has had enormous help in establishing good government from the international community and the United Nations, a pattern unlikely to recur in every African country.

> *In Central Asia, elections, even when reasonably free . . . have resulted in . . . few civil and economic liberties.*

In Central Asia, elections, even when reasonably free, as in Kyrgyzstan, have resulted in strong executives, weak legislatures and judiciaries, and few civil and economic liberties. Some countries have held no elections; there, popular autocrats hold sway. Azerbaijan's president, Gaidar Aliyev, for example, is a former head of the Soviet-era intelligence bureau, the KGB, and a former member of the Soviet Politburo. He ousted his predecessor in a coup in 1993, but most serious observers of the region suspect that if a free and fair election were held today, Aliyev would win. Even when heroes become leaders, it doesn't seem to change much. [Until 2003] Georgia [was] run by the venerated Eduard Shevardnadze, [former Soviet leader Mikhail] Gorbachev's reformist foreign minister who helped end the Cold War. Still, Shevardnadze [rigged] elections in his favor (even though he would [have] probably [won] a free one) and [ran] a country in which corruption [was] pervasive and individual liberties insecure.

Range of Illiberal Democracies

Naturally, illiberal democracy runs along a spectrum, from modest offenders such as Argentina to near-tyrannies such as Kazakhstan, with countries such as Ukraine and Venezuela in between. Along much of the spectrum, elections are rarely as free and fair as in the West today, but they do reflect popular participation in politics and support for those elected. The mixture of democracy and authoritarianism varies from country to country—Russia actually holds freer elections than most—but all contain these seemingly disparate elements. The only data base that scores countries separately on their democratic and constitutional records shows a clear rise in illiberal democracy over the last decade. In 1990 only 22 percent of democratizing countries could have been so categorized; in 1992 that figure had risen to 35 percent; in 1997 it was 50 percent, from which peak it has since declined somewhat. Still, as of [2003] close to half of the "democratizing" countries in the world are illiberal democracies.

> *Many illiberal democracies . . . have quickly and firmly turned into dictatorships. Elections in these countries merely legitimized power grabs.*

Yet some call it simply a passing phase, the growing pains that young democracies must endure. The *Economist* has argued that constitutional liberalism "is more likely to occur in a democracy." But is this commonly asserted view true? Do elections in places such as Central Asia and Africa open up political space in a country, forcing broader political, economic, and legal reforms? Or do these elections provide a cover for authoritarianism and populism? It is too soon to tell—most of these transitions are still underway—but the signs are not encouraging. Many illiberal democracies—almost all in Central Asia, for example—have quickly and firmly turned into dictatorships. Elections in these countries merely legitimized power grabs. In others, such as many in Africa, rapid moves toward democracy have undermined state authority, producing regional and ethnic challenges to central rule. Still others, such as Venezuela and Peru, retain some level of genuine democracy with lots of illiberal practices. Finally, there are cases such as Croatia and Slovakia, where an illiberal democratic system is evolving in a more constitutional and reformist direction. In these cases, the democratic element was a crucial spur to reform because it did what democracy does better than any other form of government: it threw the bums out, providing for a peaceful transfer of power from the old guard to a new regime. Note, however, that Croatia and Slovakia are both European countries with relatively high per capita incomes: $6,698 and $9,624, respectively. In general, outside Europe, illiberal democracy has not proved to be an effective path to liberal democracy.

Pakistan's Liberal Autocrat

Consider Pakistan. In October 1999, the Western world was surprised when Pakistan's army chief, General Pervez Musharraf, overthrew the freely elected prime minister, Nawaz Sharif. The surprising fact was not the coup—it was Pakistan's fourth in as many decades—but its popularity. Most Pakistanis were happy to be rid of eleven years of sham democracy. During that period, Sharif and his predecessor, Benazir Bhutto, abused their office for personal gain, packed the courts with political cronies, fired local governments, allowed Islamic fundamentalists to enact draconian laws, and plundered the state coffers. The headline of an essay in one of Pakistan's leading newspapers in January 1998 described the state of the country: "Fascist Democracy: Grab Power, Gag Opposition." Western, particularly American, newspapers had a very different reaction. Almost all righteously condemned the coup. During the 2000 presidential campaign, George W. Bush confessed to not remembering the name of the new Pakistani leader, but said that he would "bring stability to the region." The *Washington Post* immediately denounced him for uttering such heresies about a dictator.

> *If genuine liberalization and even democracy come to Pakistan it will come not because of its history of illiberal democracy but because it stumbled on a liberal autocrat.*

Two years later and with the transforming events of September 11 on his side, Musharraf had pursued a path of radical political, social, educational, and economic reform that even his supporters would not have predicted. Few elected politicians in Pakistan supported his moves. Musharraf has been able to promote these policies precisely because he did not have to run for office and cater to the interests of feudal bosses, Islamic militants, and regional chieftains. There was no guarantee that a dictator would do what Musharraf did. But in Pakistan no elected politician would have acted as boldly, decisively, and effectively as he did. As of this writing, Musharraf seems somewhat more autocratic and somewhat less liberal than he seemed at first flush. Yet he remains determined to modernize and secularize his country, although he is facing opposition from many feudal and religious factions in Pakistani society. Reforming Pakistan—economically and politically—is a near-impossible task. But . . . if genuine liberalization and even democracy come to Pakistan it will come not because of its history of illiberal democracy but because it stumbled on a liberal autocrat.

Populist Autocracy

Current concerns about elected autocrats in Russia, Central Asia, and Latin America would not have surprised nineteenth-century liberals such as John Stuart Mill. Mill opened his classic *On Liberty* by noting that as countries became democratic, people tended to believe that "too much importance had been attached to the limitation of [governmental] power itself. That . . . was a response against rulers whose interests were opposed to those of the people." Once the people were themselves in charge, caution was unnecessary; "The nation did not need to be protected against its own will." As if confirming Mill's fears, Aleksandr Lukashenko, after being elected president of Belarus overwhelmingly in a free 1994 election, when asked about limiting his powers, said, "There will be no dictatorship. I am of the people, and I am going to be for the people."

The tension between constitutional liberalism and democracy centers on the scope of governmental authority. Constitutional liberalism is about the limitation of power; democracy is about its accumulation and use. For this reason, many eighteenth- and nineteenth-century liberals saw democracy as a force that could undermine liberty. The tendency for a democratic government to believe it has absolute sovereignty (that is, power) can result in the centralization of authority, often by extraconstitutional means and with grim results. What you end up with is little different from a dictatorship, albeit one that has greater legitimacy.

Over the past decade, elected governments claiming to represent the people have steadily encroached on the powers and rights of other elements in society, a usurpation that is both horizontal (from other branches of the national government) and vertical (from regional and local authorities as well as private businesses and other nongovernmental groups such as the press). . . . Even a bona fide reformer such as former Argentine president Carlos Menem passed close to 300 presidential decrees in his eight years in office, about three times as many as were passed by all previous Argentine presidents put together, going back to 1853. Kyrgyzstan's Askar Akayev, elected with 60 percent of the vote, proposed enhancing his powers in a referendum that passed easily in 1996. His powers now include appointing all top officials except the prime minister, although he can dissolve parliament if it turns down three of his nominees for that post.

Horizontal usurpation is more obvious, but vertical usurpation is more common. Over the past three decades, elected governments in India and Pakistan routinely disbanded state legislatures on flimsy grounds, placing regions under direct rule of the central government. In a less dramatic but typical move, the elected government of the Central African Republic ended the long-standing independence of its university system, making it part of the central state apparatus. The widespread use of security forces to intimidate journalists—from Peru to Ukraine to the Philippines—systematically weakens a crucial check on governmental power. In Latin America even a supposedly reformist democrat, like Peru's Alberto Toledo, has routinely used his presidential powers to intimidate political opponents.

> *Constitutional liberalism is about the limitation of power; democracy is about its accumulation and use.*

Usurpation is particularly widespread in Latin America and the former Soviet Union, perhaps because the states in these regions feature, for the most part, presidential systems. These systems tend to produce leaders who believe that they speak for the people—even when they have been elected by no more than a plurality. As the political scientist Juan Linz has pointed out, Salvador Allende was elected to the Chilean presidency in 1970 with only 36 percent of the vote. In similar circumstances in a parliamentary system, a prime minister would have had to share power in a coalition government. Presidents appoint cabinets of cronies, rather than senior party figures, maintaining few internal checks on their power. And when their views conflict with those of the legislature, or even the courts, presidents tend to "go to the nation," bypassing the dreary tasks of bargaining and coalition-building. Scholars debate the merits of presidential versus parliamentary forms of government, and certainly usurpation can occur under either, absent well-developed alternate centers of power such as strong legislatures, courts, political parties, and regional governments, as well as independent universities and news media. Many countries in Latin America actually combine presidential systems with proportional representation, producing populist leaders and multiple parties—an unstable combination.

The Dangers of Strong Governments

Governments that usurp powers do not end up producing well-run, stable countries. A strong government is different from an effective government; in fact, the two may be contradictory. Africa has power-hungry and ineffective states. The United States has a government with limited powers and yet is a highly effective state. Confusing these two concepts has led many Western governments and scholars to encourage the creation of strong and centralized states in the Third World. Leaders in these countries have argued that they need the authority to break down feudalism, split entrenched coalitions, override vested interests, and bring order to chaotic societies. There is some truth to this concern, but it confuses legitimate government with one that is all-powerful. Governments that are limited, and thus seen as legitimate, can usually maintain order and pursue tough policies, albeit slowly, by building coalitions. The key test of a government's legitimacy is tax collection, because it requires not vast police forces but rather voluntary compliance with laws. No government has a large enough police force to coerce people to pay their taxes. Yet Third World governments have abysmally low tax-collection rates. This is because they—and their policies—lack legitimacy.

The case of Russia is . . . instructive. Since the fall of the Soviet Union, Western academics and journalists have fretted loudly about the weakness of the Russian state. Their analysis was based mostly on its inability to collect taxes—a dubious measure, since the Russian state had never done so before and thus was taking on a new task in the post-Soviet era. In fact, the Russian state after Soviet communism was still very powerful. It was, however, corrupt and widely viewed as illegitimate. Today, after years of stability and some important reforms (under [Russian president Vladimir] Putin), the Russian government collects taxes at about the level of most European countries. Still, the earlier academic worrying had real effects on public policy. Western statesmen were far too understanding of [former Russian president Boris] Yeltsin's various decrees and power grabs. They believed him when he said that the central government was under siege and needed help.

> ***Over the past decade, elected governments claiming to represent the people have steadily encroached on the powers and rights of other elements in society.*

As only a politician can, Putin ended this academic debate. Within months of his inauguration, he successfully reasserted the Kremlin's power against every competing authority and demonstrated that the old Soviet institutions have life in them yet. When formal measures were not enough he used his powers of "persuasion." Legislators and judges who refuse to vote with the Kremlin are denied their salaries and perks (the Russian parliament does not have control over its own salaries, let alone over other governmental funds). This explains why the upper house of parliament was willing to vote for the reduction of its own power and size, not an everyday occurrence in politics. As for taxes, the government collected 100 percent of its target tax revenues in 2000. It turns out that the problem in Russia was not that the state was sick but that Yeltsin was. With a living, breathing president, big government is back. This might prove to be an unfortunate development; the weakening of the central state was a needed corrective to the Soviet superstate. . . .

If the first source of abuse in a democratic system comes from elected autocrats, the second comes from the people themselves. James Madison explained in the *Federalist Papers* that "the danger of oppression" in a democracy came from "the majority of the community." [A French observer in postcolonial America, Alexis de] Tocqueville warned of the "tyranny of the majority," writing, "The very essence of democratic government consists in the absolute sovereignty of the majority." This problem, alive and urgent to Madison and Tocqueville, may seem less important in the West today because elaborate protections for individual and minority rights exist here. But in many developing countries, the experience of democracy over the past few decades has been one in which majorities have—often quietly, sometimes noisily—eroded separations of power, undermined human rights, and corrupted long-standing traditions of tolerance and fairness.

Organizations to Contact

The editors have compiled the following list of organizations concerned with the issues debated in this book. The descriptions are derived from materials provided by the organizations. All have publications or information available for interested readers. The list was compiled on the date of publication of the present volume; the information provided here may change. Be aware that many organizations take several weeks or longer to respond to inquiries, so allow as much time as possible.

American Civil Liberties Union (ACLU)
125 Broad St., 18th Fl., New York, NY 10004-2400
(888) 567-ACLU
e-mail: aclu@aclu.org • Web site: www.aclu.org

Founded in 1920, the ACLU is a national organization that works to defend civil liberties in the United States. It publishes various materials on the Bill of Rights, including regular in-depth reports, the triannual newsletter *Civil Liberties*, and a set of handbooks on individual rights.

Amnesty International (AI)
322 Eighth Ave., New York, NY 10001
(212) 807-8400 • fax: (212) 463-9193
e-mail: admin-us@aiusa.org • Web site: www.amnesty.org

Founded in 1961 and made up of over 1.8 million members in over 150 countries, AI is dedicated to promoting human rights worldwide. AI maintains an extremely active news Web site, distributes a large annual report on the state of human rights in countries throughout the world (as well as numerous special reports on specific human rights issues), and publishes the *Wire*, its monthly magazine.

Cato Institute
1000 Massachusetts Ave. NW, Washington, DC 20001-5403
(202) 842-0200 • fax: (202) 842-3490
Web site: www.cato.org

The Cato Institute is a libertarian public policy institute that supports capitalism, free trade, and civil liberties. The institute publishes the quarterly magazine *Regulation*, the bimonthly *Cato Policy Report*, and numerous books.

Children's Rights Information Network (CRIN)
c/o Save the Children, 1 St. John's Lane, London EC1M 4AR UK
+44-20-7012-6865 • fax: +44-20-7012-6952
e-mail: info@crin.org • Web site: www.crin.org

CRIN is an international network of children's rights organizations united in their support for the United Nations Convention on the Rights of the Child. The network publishes information on children's rights, including

113

Towards Transnational Cooperation for Children and *The Moral Status of Children: Essays on the Rights of the Child.*

Global Exchange
2017 Mission St., No. 303, San Francisco, CA 94110
(800) 497-1994 • fax: (415) 255-7498
e-mail: gx-info@globalexchange.org
Web site: www.globalexchange.org

Global Exchange is a nonprofit organization that promotes social justice, environmental sustainability, and grassroots activism on international human rights issues. Global Exchange produces various books, videos, and other educational programs and materials concerning human rights.

Heritage Foundation
214 Massachusetts Ave. NE, Washington, DC 20002-4999
(202) 546-4400 • fax: (202) 546-8328
e-mail: info@heritage.org • Web site: www.heritage.org

The Heritage Foundation is a conservative public policy think tank that addresses issues pertaining to terrorism and civil liberties, among other topics. It publishes regular e-mail briefings as part of its *PolicyWire* newsletter service, as well as other articles, newletters, and special reports. Many of its publications can be accessed online.

Human Rights Watch (HRW)
350 Fifth Ave., 34th Fl., New York, NY 10118-3299
(212) 290-4700 • fax: (212) 736-1300
e-mail: hrwnyc@hrw.org • Web site: www.hrw.org

In 1988 several large regional organizations dedicated to promoting human rights merged to form HRW, a global watchdog group. HRW publishes numerous books, policy papers, and special reports (including a comprehensive annual report), sponsors an annual film festival on human rights issues, and files lawsuits on behalf of those whose rights are violated.

International Committee of the Red Cross (ICRC)
Washington, D.C., Regional Delegation
2100 Pennsylvania Ave. NW, Suite 545, Washington, DC 20037
(202) 293-9430 • fax: (202) 293-9431
e-mail: washington.was@icrc.org • Web site: www.icrc.org

Founded in 1863, the ICRC is one of the few organizations to have won the Nobel Peace Prize (and did so on three occasions: in 1917, 1944, and 1963). It was the ICRC that led to the creation of the Geneva Conventions on the treatment of prisoners of war, the wounded, and medical personnel, among others. Today, the ICRC continues its mission by investigating reports of human rights violations, assisting in disaster relief, and working on behalf of those who are wounded or imprisoned in wartime.

International Labour Office (ILO)
Washington Branch, 1828 L St. NW, Washington, DC 20036
(202) 653-7652 • fax: (202) 653-7687
e-mail: ilowbo@aol.com • Web site: www.ilo.org

The ILO works to promote basic human rights by enhancing opportunities for those who are excluded from meaningful salaried employment. The ILO pioneered such landmarks of industrial society as the eight-hour workday, maternity protection, and workplace safety regulations. It runs the ILO Publications Bureau, which publishes various policy statements and background information on all aspects of employment.

International Society for Peace and Human Rights (ISPHR)
University of Alberta
Box 40, 2-900, 8900-114 St., Edmonton, AB T6G 2J7 Canada
Web site: www.peaceandhumanrights.org

A new organization created by students and faculty at the University of Alberta, the ISPHR promotes human rights activism on an international scale. It hosts regular events in Canada and publishes articles on specific human rights issues. The ISPHR is best known for its Iraq Adopt-a-Town Campaign, whereby citizens of several major Canadian cities "adopt" and coordinater funds to support specific towns in war-torn regions of Iraq.

John Humphrey Centre for Peace and Human Rights
Box/CP 11661, Edmonton, AB T5J 3K8 Canada
(780) 452-2638 • fax: (780) 482-1519
e-mail: info@johnhumphreycentre.org
Web site: www.johnhumphreycentre.org

Named after the Canadian attorney who played a formative role in drafting the United Nations' 1948 Universal Declaration of Human Rights, this organization supports human rights scholarship and provides resources for students interested in studying international human rights law. Among other things, the Web site features a youth guide to the Canadian Charter of Rights and Freedoms.

United Nations Association of the USA (UNA-USA)
801 Second Ave., 2nd Fl., New York, NY 10017-4706
(212) 907-1300 • fax: (212) 682-9185
e-mail: unany@igc.apc.org • Web site: www.unausa.org

UNA-USA is the largest grassroots foreign policy organization in the United States and the nation's leading center of policy research on the United Nations and global issues. It works with the United Nations to identify better ways in which the international community can use its resources to respond to pressing human needs, such as international counterterrorism, emergency relief, and human rights activism. It publishes the quarterly newspaper *Inter Dependent*, the annual volume *A Global Agenda: Issues Before the General Assembly of the United Nations*, and the *Washington Weekly Report*.

United Nations Children's Fund (UNICEF)
U.S. Committee, 333 E. Thirty-eighth St., New York, NY 10016
(212) 686-5522 • fax: (212) 779-1679
e-mail: information@unicefusa.org • Web site: www.unicef.org

The United States is one of thirty-seven nations that raises money for UNICEF, an organization that provides health care, clean water, improved nutrition, and education to millions of children in more than

160 countries and territories. UNICEF also works to spread awareness about the status of the world's children. Its publications include an annual report titled *The State of the World's Children,* and presentation papers from international child labor conferences.

U.S. Department of State, Counterterrorism Office
PA/PL, Rm. 2206, 2201 C St. NW, Washington, DC 20520
(202) 647-6575
Web site: www.state.gov/s/ct

The U.S. Department of State's counterterrorism office is responsible for coordinating international efforts to fight terrorism. The office's Web site includes pages dealing with current events, patterns of global terrorism, homeland security, and other issues pertaining to counterterrorism efforts.

U.S. Naval Base at Guantánamo Bay, Cuba
PSC 1005, Box 25, FPO AE 09593

The U.S. Naval Base at Guantánamo Bay hosts hundreds of accused Taliban and al Qaeda fighters imprisoned during the Afghanistan War of 2001. Human rights groups argue that these detainees have been denied access to the U.S. criminal justice system and subjected to "stress and duress" interrogation techniques. In *Rasul v. Bush* (2004), the U.S. Supreme Court sided with the detainees and ruled that they have the right to challenge their status in U.S. civilian courts.

Bibliography

Books

Alison Brysk, ed.	*Globalization and Human Rights.* Berkeley and Los Angeles: University of California Press, 2002.
Jack Donnelly	*Universal Human Rights in Theory and Practice.* Ithaca, NY: Cornell University Press, 2002.
William Driscoll, Joseph Zompetti, and Susan W. Zompetti, eds.	*The International Criminal Court.* Budapest, Hungary: Central European University Press, 2004.
Dore Gold	*Tower of Babble: How the United Nations Has Fueled Global Chaos.* New York: Crown Forum, 2004.
Amy Gutman, ed.	*Human Rights as Politics and Idolatry.* Princeton, NJ: Princeton University Press, 2003.
Laura Hapke	*Sweatshop: The History of an American Idea.* Piscataway, NJ: Rutgers University Press, 2004.
Micheline R. Ishay	*The History of Human Rights.* Berkeley and Los Angeles: University of California Press, 2004.
Micheline R. Ishay, ed.	*The Human Rights Reader.* Abingdon, UK: Routledge, 1997.
David Kennedy	*The Dark Sides of Virtue: Reassessing International Humanitarianism.* Princeton, NJ: Princeton University Press, 2004.
Isaac Kramnick, ed.	*The Portable Enlightenment Reader.* New York: Viking, 1995.
Chris Mackey and Greg Miller	*The Interrogators: Inside the Secret War Against al Qaeda.* New York: Little, Brown, 2004.
Thomas Pogge	*World Poverty and Human Rights.* Cambridge, UK: Polity, 2002.
Robert J.S. Ross	*Slaves to Fashion: Poverty and Abuse in the New Sweatshops.* Ann Arbor: University of Michigan Press, 2004.
William A. Schabas	*An Introduction to the International Criminal Court.* Cambridge: Cambridge University Press, 2004.
Natan Sharansky, with Ron Dermer	*The Case for Democracy.* New York: PublicAffairs, 2004.

117

Henry Shue — *Basic Rights: Subsistence, Affluence, and U.S. Foreign Policy.* Princeton, NJ: Princeton University Press, 1996.

Peter Singer — *One World: The Ethics of Globalization.* 2nd ed. New Haven, CT: Yale University Press, 2004.

Stephen C. Smith — *Ending Global Poverty: A Guide to What Works.* New York: Palgrave Macmillan, 2005.

Joseph E. Stiglitz — *Globalization and Its Discontents.* New York: W.W. Norton, 2003.

Fareed Zakaria — *The Future of Freedom: Illiberal Democracy at Home and Abroad.* New York: W.W. Norton, 2003.

Periodicals

Reed Brody — "Prisoners Who Disappear," *International Herald Tribune*, October 12, 2004.

Clarence J. Dias — "No Development Without Human Rights," *UN Chronicle*, September 2002.

Tom Freeman — "Mission Impossible?" *New Statesman*, October 11, 2004.

Georgette Gagnon and Brenda Dinnick — "Sudan: Words Are Not Enough," *Globe and Mail* (Canada), June 11, 2004.

Michael Gilgannon — "Globalization Proceeds Without Practical Ethical Guides," *National Catholic Reporter*, December 17, 2004.

Neve Gordon — "Strategic Violations: The Outsourcing of Human Rights Abuses," *Humanist*, September 2003.

Elise Keppler — "Grave Crimes: Darfur and the International Criminal Court," *World Today*, January 1, 2005.

Edith M. Lederer — "'No Going Back' on Fight for Women's Equality," *Deseret News*, March 2005.

Dahlia Lithwick and Julia Turner — "A Guide to the Patriot Act," *Slate*, September 8–13, 2003.

Heather Mac Donald — "Torturing the Evidence: The Truth About Guantanamo," *Weekly Standard*, January 24, 2005.

Tibor R. Machan — "Globalization Versus Imperialism," *Reason*, April 1, 2002.

Mark Mazower — "The Strange Triumph of Human Rights," *New Statesman*, February 4, 2002.

Sergio Vieira de Mello — "Their Dignity Will Be as Mine, as It Is Yours: Human Rights and the Role of the United Nations," *UN Chronicle*, December 2002.

Rob Nelson — "Seeing Is Believing: Handicams, Human Rights and the News," *Mother Jones*, September 2003.

Timothy Noah	"Everybody Hates Peacekeeping," *Slate*, October 21, 2003.
Kate O'Beirne	"Their Brothers' Keepers: The Conservative Shade of Human Rights Activists," *National Review*, June 30, 2003.
Alex Otieno	"The Role of Education in Promoting Health and Human Rights," *UN Chronicle*, June 2004.
Leslie Palti	"Combating Terrorism While Protecting Human Rights," *UN Chronicle*, December 2004.
Robert Poe	"Patriot Games," *Slate*, March 8, 2005.
Ramesh Ponnuru	"1984 in 2003? Fears About the Patriot Act Are Misguided," *National Review*, June 2, 2003.
Ramesh Ponnuru	"Watching the Watchmen," *National Review*, April 8, 2002.
Kenneth Roth	"Human Rights in the War on Terrorism," *Boston Globe*, September 22, 2004.
David Ruffin	"Darfur: Genocide in Plain View," *Crisis*, January 1, 2005.
Marcela Sanchez	"More Is Not Always Better for Human Rights," *Washington Post*, February 3, 2005.
Jeremy Seabrook	"In the Shadow of the Torturer," *New Internationalist*, August 2004.
Kate Taylor	"What Is International Law?" *Slate*, October 15, 2002.
J.M. Vorster	"Racism, Xenophobia and Human Rights," *Ecumenical Review*, July 2002.

Internet Sources

Amnesty International	*Annual Report.* www.amnesty.org.
Human Rights Watch	*World Report 2004.* http://hrw.org.
Robert Scheer	"Throwing It All Away," *Salon.com*, November 21, 2001. http://dir.salon.com.
U.S. Department of State	*Annual Report 2004.* www.state.gov.

Index